FREEZE FRAME

For Dad, Sue and Liam.
Three uniquely special people.

Contents

Foreword

If you are going to get yourself into uncomfortable, difficult, even dangerous circumstances, try to ensure that your companion is a wildlife cameraman. It is a policy that I have practised for many years, and it has served me remarkably well. Such people know how to repair car engines with bits and pieces collected from the surrounding wilderness; how to turn the most disgusting ingredients into something edible; how to laugh after being charged by a polar bear; how to wheedle their way past the most obstructive of customs officers; and how to deal with surly, drunken soldiers carrying loaded rifles, who clearly don't like you and with whom you don't share a single intelligible word.

Doug Allan is one of the most gifted of these exceptional people. I first met him more than 30 years ago in circumstances that for me were extremely dramatic but for him, everyday. I was standing on the edge of the sea ice in Antarctica looking down at the black water. A head materialised many feet down, slowly rose, surrounded by bubbles, and broke the surface. It was Doug. He had been swimming for the past half hour beneath the ice on which I was standing. He removed the mouthpiece of his breathing apparatus and said, in the Scottish accent with which I was to become very familiar, "I want to make natural history films for television. How do I start?"

Since that time it has been my extraordinary luck to have worked with him many times in many places, some of them very hot, which he endures, most of them cripplingly cold, which he loves. He is not, as will be clear from what follows, as other men. He cheerfully endures conditions more uncomfortable and for longer periods than anyone I know. He has a unique sense of humour, which means he often sees the funny side of things that until then you had failed to recognise. He has an uncanny understanding of animals, ranging from tiny birds to gigantic whales, that tells him what the animal is about to do before it does it – and so enables him to move his camera to get a breathtaking, perfectly composed shot.

And he is a wonderful companion – which is perhaps the quality you most need in the circumstances described in the pages that follow.

David Attenborough

A summer day on the ice.
David Attenborough and Doug Allan,
filming in Svalbard for *The Life of Mammals*.

It All Began in the Womb

It wasn't easy being a twin. At the root of my character was probably simply the desire to be different. So I dived first into books, then under water.

It was the sixties, the sea and space were the frontiers, Cousteau and Hass were on the box. If you want to go Freudian, here was my subconscious means of escape. On the family package holidays to Spain in the mid-sixties, the Mediterranean was the perfect place to start snorkelling.

I've only ever made three career decisions in my life, and for all of them I followed my heart as much as my head. When I graduated in marine biology in 1973, I only wanted to pursue a further degree if it involved diving. None was offered. So I came out of academia and instead dived for freshwater pearls in Scotland, scraped up enough savings to go and work with some Cambridge University biologists in the central Red Sea and then ran a dive school in Jersey. I hadn't even picked up a camera at that point.

While with the dive school in 1975, I read an article in a magazine by a scientific diver recently returned from the Antarctic. I tracked down the address for the British Antarctic Survey (BAS) and applied for a post. A month later I had an interview. A week later, two letters arrived. The first said that my application to be a diver with BAS had been unsuccessful; the other was an invitation back to the Red Sea. That's where I was, in 28°C water, when a telex from BAS came in: "Unexpected vacancy Signy island. Do you wish 12 month posting?" Thus was decision number two made. Within a month, in February 1976, I was on the BAS ship from Punta Arenas to the South Orkneys. Out of the frying pan into the fridge.

I spent the next nine years with BAS, doing four winters and nine summers in the Antarctic, which included one unbroken spell of two and a half years. I was a diver, scientist, photographer and finally base commander. After the initial misunderstanding at my interview, BAS and I developed a great relationship. To say the experiences changed my life would be an understatement. To a very large degree it made me the person I am today. I did three contracts with BAS, each a little more challenging, each uniquely satisfying.

I had all the encouragement I needed to improve my photography. Indeed it was a chance meeting with David Attenborough in the Antarctic in February 1981 that was a major step in my making the third decision. That was to take a movie camera on my next BAS assignment, to Halley station. This was a chance to overwinter with emperor penguins, and on my return, I sold some of the footage to the BBC for a series it was making about birds. This led to more filming, and in 1985, I left BAS to try to follow the road to full-time filming.

I knew from the start the films I wanted to make – an underwater one about research diving on Signy and a second about Weddell seals. BAS again helped enormously with logistics. I offered the ideas to Survival Anglia and so was back south in 1987. I was super-enthusiastic but also super-naïve. The stress of shooting the films over nine months was intense. Bear in mind

this was film not video. Because of the isolation of the Antarctic winter, I had no feedback on content or quality. I came out in December with 130 rolls of film and no idea how any of it looked until the cans were processed and I sat with the producer six weeks later.

But it did all work out, and I've been filming in the poles and around the world ever since. I've had the great good fortune to work with some of the best in the business. Films are truly collaborative efforts, and when all the participants are in full song, the whole is for sure greater than the sum of the parts. *Life in the Freezer, Arctic Kingdom: Life at the Edge, Polar Bear Special, The Blue Planet, A Boy Among Polar Bears, Planet Earth, Human Planet, Ocean Giants, Frozen Planet, Operation Iceberg* and *Forces of Nature* – all were made possible by truly talented production teams.

I claim never to be competitive, which makes those who know me laugh out loud. I'd prefer to be thought of as having tenacity – a characteristic that has a streak of doggedness to it, and so is a different beast from mere patience.

Patience is sitting, waiting and watching for days.

Tenacity is sitting, waiting and watching for days in the blowing snow.

Wildlife filming, on the other hand, is sitting, waiting and watching for days in the blowing snow, but at least you're being paid for it.

This book had a gradual genesis. While filming has been at the heart of my career, I've always seen the written word as having a permanence that moving pictures seldom do. There's something about the greater investment of time and effort required by the reader compared to the viewer, how books leave space for your imagination to reach into, while television does most of it for you. Over the years, I had fresh spurts of enthusiasm with lots of plans and talks, interspersed with long periods of laziness, frustration and guilt. The angst of the empty page was all too real. Diving and filming are easy, writing is difficult. In the end, two things took me to the tipping point.

I watched Sue Flood produce her lovely book *Cold Places*, then recalled the quotation by the climber Yvon Chouinard, whose friend had warned him what it was like to write a book. "I've decided that all this sitting around and writing is bullshit. The only thing that counts is the self-discipline." In my case, it was all the sitting around and talking that was bullshit. The time had come to get the words down.

Every picture tells a story. I've just given the ones in this book a chance to tell theirs. My hope is that these images and the stories behind them will help explain what drives me and others in the wildlife-filming community, give a greater understanding of the art and practices of film-making with animals, and offer intimate insights about the animals themselves and the wild places where they live.

May you leave with a deeper admiration for all the natural wonders that we still have but aware of how much we should be doing to make sure they remain.

Doug Allan

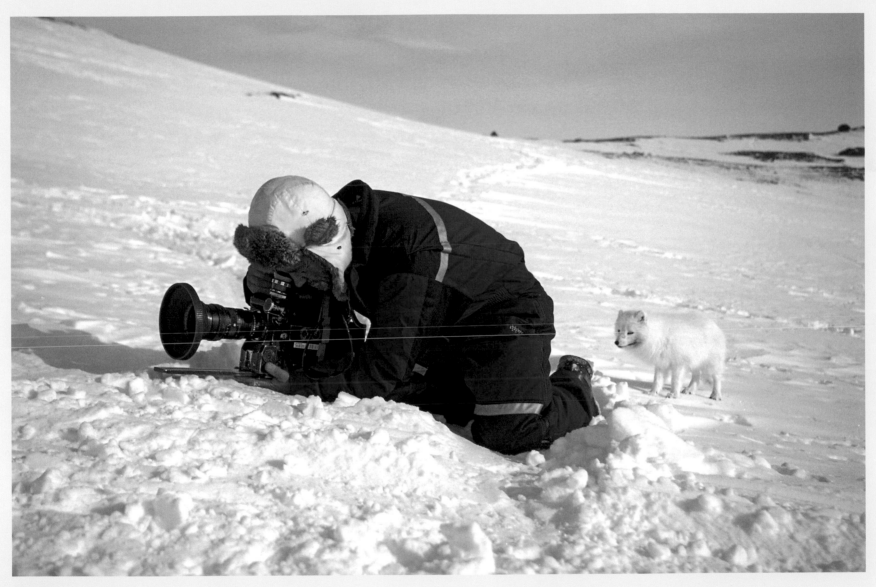

It's behind you…
I'd asked Jason to take a picture of me filming the Arctic foxes on a Svalbard shoot for *The Life of Mammals*. I assumed he'd include the pair 3 metres in front of me, not this one that came up from behind. There's a message here for all wildlife photographers.

FREEZE FRAME

CAMERAWORK

Bring Me Back a Blizzard

The challenge to you, dear reader, is this. Can you tell how cold it actually was when this picture was taken? I ask because absolute cold is often a very difficult concept to show.

"Make sure you get me a blizzard" is a frequent production request – but usually not by anyone who's actually been in a real blizzard. For in true blizzard conditions, it's a white-out: contrast is zero, visibility is down to metres, and you might as well film with half a ping-pong ball over the lens for all you'll see. No, what they mean is "Please see if you can film some beautifully backlit drifting snow, with the sun low in the sky, so I can write the commentary emphasising the chill of the Arctic/Antarctic winter."

I've had people suggest I go to the high Arctic in January because "that's when it's coldest and we'll get the most dramatic shots", forgetting that above 75 degrees north it's pitch black most of the time through January because the sun is below the horizon 24 hours a day.

The truth is that below about -20°C it all looks the same. There's no melt and the snow is dry rather than sticky. So it blows around easily. But the difficulties of filming increase dramatically if you're out in colder than -20°C. Most gear will work OK down to -15, but as you sink towards -25 or even -35, the challenges mount. Batteries die faster, electronics become less reliable, flexible power or sound cables snap like dry spaghetti. And there's a very real danger of frost damage to the cameraperson as well as to the gear.

Unless I want to cover some behaviour that happens only in late winter (such as bears coming out of their dens), I try to avoid going to the far north on a serious shooting expedition until late March or early April. It's still cold but not creatively crippling cold. It's not a damp chill but invigoratingly dry. There's still a sunset and a sunrise, and so you have the best of low-light periods. And April is when the ringed seals give birth, which means the polar bears are starting to hunt more actively. The sea ice is still solid, you're unlikely to drop through a crack, and the snow's still squeaky hard and easy to drive or walk over. My perfect temperature is -18°C. ∎

A breeze. Signy sea ice 15 May, -5°C and 25 knots of wind making it -17°C equivalent. There had been a lot of light snowfall the previous day – perfect for the creation of 'blizzard conditions' whenever the wind picked up. This photo sells the most as a picture of bleak and bitter polar landscape, despite it actually being taken on the 'warmest' day.

Previous page
White-wear. The only way I could approach even remotely close to wary Baikal seal pups on the ice was by wearing a white camouflaged anorak and crouching down so that I was hidden behind the white sail of Misch's little sledge (see page 48).

Chilly. Signy sea ice, 61 degrees south, 18 June, -12°C with
20 knots of wind giving -27°C equivalent, but not much snow
to blow about. Very pretty but a failure as far as being
a cold-looking picture.

Cold. Kong Karl's Land, 79 degrees north, 14 March, -30°C
with 20 knots of wind making a windchill of -52°C equivalent.
The sun had absolutely no warmth at all. My camera took one
shot before giving up the ghost with the cold.

Showtime on the Slopes

7 April, 4.50am. Time to rise. Beyond the cabin window, only occasional and erratic slivers of spindrift snake over the sea ice – that's good, the wind has dropped. In the bunk below, Jason stirs, but it's going to take a full-strength coffee to actually wake him. We make a good team: I'm a morning man, but he'll make supper in about 15 hours when I'm knackered after a day's filming.

I pause at the door before heading out for a pee. We had two bear visitors last night, and one or both might be back. They weren't aggressive, just curious. There must be a scent trail miles long from our cabin when we're cooking. We scared both of them away simply by clapping and shouting, and it's unlikely they'd now be lying in wait for us. But it wouldn't do to surprise them if they had come back and were sleeping just around the corner.

As the coffee brews, I reflect on how it's been a long haul at this location. Tenacity is just patience showing its teeth, and for sure it's been tough covering the ground just looking for bear dens.

We came to Kong Karl's Land because, 25 years ago, when the last two Norwegian scientists worked here, they found 20 dens in one valley. This should be a bear Mecca, a location offering exciting new ▶

Solitude. Some of the loveliest moments were as we headed back across the wind-glazed snow slopes in the late evening. The nearest people on the planet were about 200km away.

Above left
Bear Corner – the nameplate on the cabin. Some nights we'd have several polar bears come nosing around.

Home. There's a saying among polar people: "Any fool can be uncomfortable." It might look bleak, but the Kong Karl's Land hut was one of the warmest, best-designed cabins I've ever used as a filming base. It was built in 1937.

Bear view. Now you can see what I mean about Bjørnehjørnet being a good name for the cabin. The bear was just the other side of the window.

Scary. The black pistol was our main deterrent for bears that came too close. It fired a flare that went off with a mighty bang. The Magnum 45 was for a really serious bear. I'm proud to say I've never used it.

▶ sequences for *Planet Earth*. But for 23 days we've searched the slopes in vain, finding only one mother and cub, in a spot impossible to film. Then yesterday we had our break.

We walked up one valley in the morning, and coming back in the late afternoon saw a dark hole in what had been an unbroken slope of virgin snow, with a scattering of pawprints around it – exactly what we had been searching for, a den site with a newly emerged bear. As quickly as we could, we dug our blind – a hole in the snow about 2 metres by 2 metres, just big enough for the pair of us to stand in with the large camera on the tripod. We built a high wall of snow blocks all round to keep us hidden from the bear. She'd smell us if the wind was wrong. She might hear us as well, but if we stayed mostly out of sight, she'd probably accept us. If she's still there, today might bring fulfilment – or bitter disappointment.

Before leaving the cabin, I double-check that we have everything we'll need – camera batteries, binoculars, spare gloves, sunglasses, thermos, chocolate and an explosive-flare pistol that I'll use if a bear does come too close. It's good that we hauled most of the heavy camera gear down on the sledges a week ago. Not much wind this morning, ▶

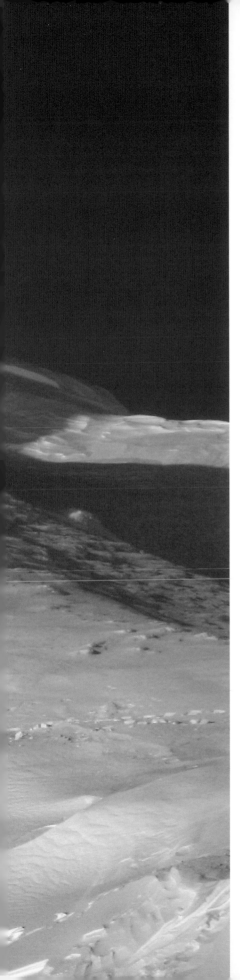

Snow hide. As the mum and her cubs became accustomed to us down the slope, we reduced the height of the wall around our filming hole. The den entrance is about 90 metres farther up the slope.

Cubbyhole. This is the den entrance viewed from the filming position. You can see old footprints half-covered in drifted snow where the mum and cubs have been out. But all tracks lead back to the hole – they're all still in there.

▶ but it's still chilly, -32°C on the thermometer, with about 10 knots of wind gusting from the east. Not a problem for going down to the denning valley, as it's at our backs, though coming home tonight into the breeze, we'll have to watch for frostbite.

When we first arrived on Kong Karl's Land 23 days ago, the prospect of having to walk everywhere was frankly dreadful – so slow, so cold, so many hassles and much more effort than if we had the usual snow machines. But this is a highly protected area, and minimum disturbance for the bears was a condition for the permission. However, by now I positively enjoy the walk. I'm aware of every nuance of the snow and ice texture beneath my feet. I can hear the high-pitched calls of the black guillemots returning to the cliffs. I'm in touch with every shift of the wind. It's as if I'm ultra-tuned in to the nature of this wonderful place. I'm in bear world, living at bear speed, with bear senses. I feel very alive.

The first 4 kilometres are on the flat sea ice, but the final 500-metre haul up the slopes of the hill is always tough. The almost constant wind has blown off all the loose snow, and so it's now hard glare ice under my boots. If it wasn't for my crampons I'd be skittering and struggling. But my timing when I reach our filming position is perfect: 90 metres farther up ▶

▶ the black hole we found is just beginning to come into full sunlight. Come on girl, it's looking good. Show us you're in there. Please don't let it be a temporary den that's now empty.

Over the hours that follow, continuous movement is the only way to stay warm. So we constantly shuffle, hop, bend, stretch and rub, and alternate between cups of coffee, a rehydrated meal and a few squares of rock-hard frozen chocolate – all the time watching that hole to catch the first sign of any movement.

Five hours of watching, and then with no warning at all, I catch a glimpse so brief that I almost miss it. But the camera's locked on the hole on full zoom, and my eye's very quickly at the viewfinder. Nothing for a couple of seconds, and then an unmistakable black nose. Nose becomes muzzle, grows bigger to be full head, and in less than a minute, she has her front legs out and is resting on the snow in front of the hole, for all the world like someone leaning out of a window, elbows on the sill. She's looking straight at me, but she's not bothered. Magic. In one smooth movement she's out completely, standing up and then rolling and stretching on the snow by her den. I've just pulled out of a close-up, thinking this can't get much better, when she sets off on ▶

Jackpot. The twins peer tentatively
out from the den entrance.

▶ a long, glorious slide, sideways down the slope. Her eyes are closed. It might be because she has her muzzle pushed into the drift as she's sliding, but I'd swear it's partly in sheer pleasure.

I'm following her in the lens as she begins to head back, but when she stops and makes a couple of jaw-clap noises, I know immediately there's some action higher up. Man, we've hit the jackpot. Looking down at mum from the den entrance are two young cubs. It's all I can do to hold back a cheer – until now I've had no idea even if there were any cubs.

Clearly it's their first view of the outside world. They look very unsure of themselves, and one seems to be shivering already. When mum reaches the hole, she immediately squeezes her bulk straight back in, and they tumble after her.

The whole excursion, from mum out to all three back in, has lasted less than five minutes, but right now my sense of relief is total. I simply and absolutely know that these bears are relaxed and already accept us. The coming days will reveal more very special moments. It's showtime on the slopes, and we have the front-row seats.

Kong Karl's Land, Spitzbergen, Norway, filming for *Planet Earth*, BBC.

Outing. A beautiful sunny day, and mum's out on the slopes with her two cubs.

In mum's footsteps. The cubs are about the size of Labrador
puppies. I remember this one falling into one of mum's deep
footprints and struggling to climb out.

Birthplace. After the bears had left for the sea ice, we had a look inside the den. You can see strands of fur in the roof and claw marks made by the mother during her three-month stay.

The trek. Passing through Rombuk village in snow leopard country. Hope remains.

Sitting it out. My little cave up a side valley. Still no luck.

The Ghost Leopard

Snow leopards are the stuff of legend. When I was offered the chance to try for them, I was daunted but deep inside pleased. I always claim to prefer the hard stuff, the 'real' animals. No habituated subjects for me. Here was the ultimate challenge. Two shoots totalling 11 weeks high in the mountains of Ladakh, one in summer, the other in winter.

I didn't realise how difficult it would be. I saw only one snow leopard in all that time. She walked for ten minutes through the snow on the other face of the valley, slept for two hours, and then walked out of sight within minutes of waking up. Hardly an Emmy-winning encounter.

I probably did go a little unhinged. We had a report that snow leopards might be seen a long way up one of the remote side valleys. So I decided to try there, but I wanted to minimise the risk of disturbance. I had a tent and supplies taken in by yak and asked that no one visit me for a week. I would radio in every evening for a safety check, but I wanted to be left completely alone.

Every day I'd rise from my tent an hour before dawn, slip into my camouflaged hide on the side of the hill and wait, watch and listen for four hours. I'd come out mid-morning, rest up and then go back in at 3pm to wait, watch and listen until dark. Did I see anything of them? No. Did I feel an inner peace? No, not really. I just kept going by reminding myself of the two mantras that keep any wildlife film-maker sane.

"Remember you can only be in one place at one time." That's for when you come back to camp after a long day's search and everyone tells you that your quarry was here, in sight for most of the day.

"Remember that if you're not out there, you'll never film it." That's to keep you trying, even when the mist's down and you can barely make out the path a few metres from the hide.

Yes, I must admit it was tedious in the hide – so few other animals to watch for, so hard to stay focused. When you're in a situation like that, listening is as important as watching. The key is to tune into the natural ambience so you can detect any change. I visualise an animal (and that includes me) carrying a sphere of influence around it. When a predator is on the move, the calls of other animals near it will signal alarm. If I'm sunk deep enough into my awareness of the environment, I'll hear those subtle changes and might get a little warning. But not this time.

My brief hours in the presence of a sleepy snow leopard were my only reward for hundreds of hours of searching. There's a certain ratio of reward to filming effort that you need to stay optimistic, and I have to admit that by the end of the assignment I was well worn down.

Ladakh, India, January and August, filming for *Planet Earth*, BBC.

Signs but no sighting.
So near yet so far.

Moose Stalking

This was on a shoot in February a few hundred kilometres north of Moscow. The first plan was to find and follow wild moose through the taiga. That was a complete non-starter. The animals had such an acute sense of hearing that they were aware of us coming long before we ever saw them. We might catch a distant and fleeting glimpse of a brown body crashing through the trees a hundred metres or so in front of us, but we never had a chance to film.

Progress through the dense forest wasn't easy, as we had to do everything on skis. We'd brought the latest fancy cross-country type from the UK, narrow and designed for speed, but the snow was so soft and deep that, even with them on, we sank up to our thighs. So we started using the locally made wider style of skis, which were fine as long as you stayed upright. But it wasn't easy thrashing around with the tripod and camera, and I often lost my balance. There was just no wind-packed snow anywhere, it was all extremely soft powder. Sometimes, if it was very deep, I'd completely disappear and then have to climb back on my planks. It was like grappling with waterskis. While I cursed and struggled, the moose slipped away.

In the end we found a herder with half a dozen much more approachable moose, easier to film but about as wild as cows in a field. Even then it wasn't quite straightforward. All of his animals had an identifying nick cut in their right ears, and if you ever see that sequence, you might just notice that all the shots are from the left-hand side, using a low viewpoint. You only ever see one ear at a time, and it's always the left one.

Russia, February, filming for *Russia*, Survival Anglia.

Moulting Party

Every year there is a remarkable gathering in the high Arctic. Belugas come together by the hundreds at the head of Cunningham Inlet, where a river empties into the sea. They've come not to feed, not to mate, but to moult. Unlike other whale species, whose skin continuously flakes off and is replaced, belugas have a synchronous moult. They arrive with their skin wrinkled and yellowed, and 20 or so days later, they leave whiter and much smoother. The fresh water of the river seems to speed up the process, and the rough gravel bottom is the perfect itch-relieving surface to rub against.

I've been there several times to film, living in a tent on the high ground overlooking the river. The location promised great things from the very first time I heard about it. "Come up on 17 July," biologist Tom Smith had told me. "That's when the numbers start to build." An easy date to remember – it's my birthday.

It was almost as though the belugas had come home. When they arrived in the inlet, we'd often see them swimming around holding their heads well clear of the water – not just for a few seconds but for minutes at a time. Tom reckoned that they were checking where they were and somehow identifying this place as their river, because certainly some of the same individuals came back year after year.

With my producer Sue, I stood on the shore and watched them lying on their backs, rubbing themselves vigorously to scrape off their old skin. They took virtually no notice as long as we stood on the beach. But if we took the smallest step into the water, wholesale panic would set in. They would all swim off down the river and back to the open water of the bay. They knew that in the shallows they were vulnerable to attack by polar bears.

For *The Blue Planet* we wanted shots of them under water. So we set up a small remote camera in midstream at low water, running a cable to a monitor in a tent on the shore. As the tide rose, the belugas swam in, and eventually many were passing right next to the camera.

We were getting great close-ups, until one juvenile became too curious. Maybe he saw himself reflected in the camera lens, or perhaps he was attracted by the electronic 'noise' from the camera. But suddenly we had a sharp view of his teeth, and then the camera was off on a journey all of its own. The beluga had grabbed it and was pulling it and the cable across the riverbed. Luckily he dropped it after only a few seconds, but not before I had visions of yet another strange insurance claim for lost equipment.

Cunningham Inlet, Somerset Island, Canadian Arctic, July, filming for *Arctic Kingdom – Life at the Edge*, National Geographic.

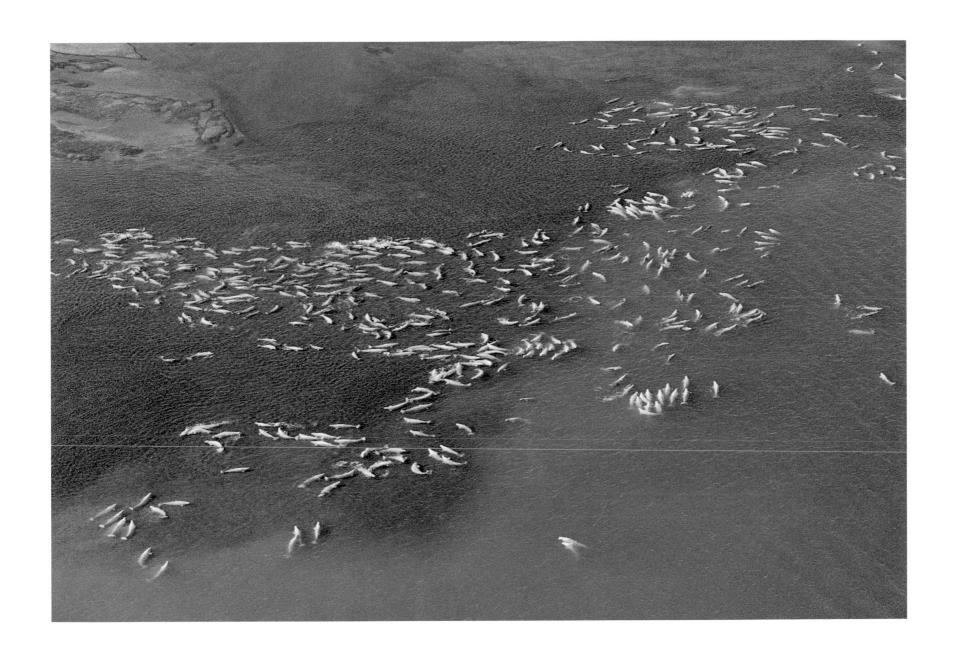

Underwater Air Nets

Bubble-netting is a humpback whale feeding technique that's often seen in Alaska. For *Life in the Freezer*, we filmed it for the first time in the Antarctic.

The humpbacks are eating krill, the tiny shrimp-like crustaceans that form a massive biomass in southern polar waters. Krill are truly the epicentre of the food web down there. But sometimes there are just not enough of them in the water to satisfy huge appetites, and a whale needs to concentrate them to make a worthwhile mouthful.

So when it finds a patch of these tiny crustaceans, a humpback dives deep below it and then swims upwards in a circle, emitting a steady stream of bubbles from its blowhole. The bubbles form a rising curtain that the krill won't swim through. In fact, they pack themselves tighter inside the bubble ring.

The krill are pushed to the surface in a concentrated ball, and the whale is right below them but coming up fast. The humpback opens its huge mouth and engulfs the ball as it breaks the surface, its baleened upper jaw fitting perfectly into the lower like a lid into a kettle.

One intriguing twist to the behaviour is that the dark, gaping mouth is not just a hugely efficient gulping machine but is also seen by the krill as the perfect place to escape into. At the very last moment, the krill actually swim right into the whale's mouth. As soon as its jaws close, the whale pushes its tongue into the roof of its mouth, squeezing seawater through the baleen plates and sieving out its tiny prey on those plates' hairy trailing edges.

The great thing about filming the behaviour was the perfection of the bubble-blowing and the predictability of where the whales would appear. We came to know exactly where to position the inflatable for the shot when the whales surfaced.

Fournier Bay, Antarctic Peninsula, January, filming for *Life in the Freezer*, BBC.

First shoot. This is the first 16mm movie camera and tripod
I ever owned, on my first proper shoot as a paid cameraman:
Signy Island in Antarctica, December 1984, filming
blue-eyed shags for the BBC series *Birds for All Seasons*.

Antediluvian Film-making

Back in the good old days, we used 16mm film cameras. The built-in exposure meter and the ability to do modest slow-motion were about the limit of a camera's sophistication. The workhorse was the Arri SR, with its quick-change magazines, rightly famed for its reliability and toughness. If you were pitching your tent on hard ground but couldn't find a hammer for the tent pegs, you could always use the Arri.

Film came in 122-metre-long rolls and had to be loaded onto the camera's magazines in total darkness. So we always had a changing bag – a close-weave, lightproof black bag with elasticated sleeves to poke your arms into. The film can and the mag went into the bag, and then you groped around inside, loading the film by touch alone. You sat down, the bag on your lap, forearms inside, with lots of grunting and hand movements in the area of your groin, and you always heard the same comments from non-film-makers who were watching.

It was a bare-hands job – wearing gloves wasn't really practical. Not difficult in normal conditions – with practice, you could do it in less than a minute. Harder at -20°C or when speed was essential. The cameraperson's worst nightmare was the crucial action happening in front of you while you were in the middle of loading the next mag.

A full mag lasted for ten minutes, or less if you were shooting slo-mo, since then you were pushing the film through the camera faster. We kept three or four loaded mags with us and maybe an extra five cans of film in our rucksacks. That was usually enough to cover what was happening, though we had our hands full if the action became really hectic and we were doing lots of slo-mo.

But while you could change mags topside in a matter of seconds, that didn't apply to under water. Down there, when you'd run your ten minutes, you had to leave your subject, swim back to the boat, put the camera and housing on board, dry it, split the housing, change the mag and put it all back together – by which time, of course, your animal had swum far away and you might not have another chance.

So the advent of electronic tape, with its 60-minute loads and big, bright viewfinders, was an advance I took to eagerly. The other big plus was video's ability to 'punch' through murky water far better than film. Low contrast and poor visibility often prevail under water, but with electronic cameras, we could bring back good images from far more difficult conditions.

The hardware of the diving equipment itself was more basic back then. When I first dived in the Antarctic in 1976, we used wetsuits – unlined, naked neoprene, seams glued and taped rather than sewn so they were effectively semi-dry, 10mm-thick rubber, with double that over the chest. They did keep you surprisingly warm for shallow dives down to about 10 metres and lasting about 45 minutes. But for multiple dives or at 25 to 30 metres, the chill factor came in with a vengeance. It was like diving wearing only a layer of tissue paper. You could feel the lack of insulation as the neoprene was squeezed and thinned because of the water pressure. Today I'm all for wimpiness and a full drysuit. Though I still prefer wet hands and head for ease of putting on and pulling off gloves and hood.

Of course, the biggest difference between the electronic image-gathering now and film back then was that there was no feedback with film until it was developed. For most shoots in remote ▶

Tight squeeze. The dive holes we drilled through the Ross Sea ice at McMurdo were only just big enough for the underwater cameras we were taking down.

Ready to go. I'm on the ice edge 32 years ago, about to make a dive. Rugged beard, wetsuit, Fenzy adjustable buoyancy lifejacket, Nikon F2 with 24mm lens, Oceanic housing, Subsea flash. Who'd have thought I'd still be selling those underwater shots today?

▶ locations, that meant we'd go there, film our subjects and return to Bristol with no absolute certainty of what was on the film.

Composition, exposure, focus, having all the shots the editor needed to put together the sequence story – you saw all those only weeks later when sitting down with the producer and editor to look at your raw 'rushes' after they had come back from the laboratory. Yes, it could be absolutely nerve-racking.

I learned the hard way how my time sense goes awry when something exciting is unfolding in front of the lens. Time seems to become stretched in my head. As I watched my shots in the viewing theatre, I realised that too many of them were too short for the editor to use effectively; I had been switching the camera off too soon.

Then another, more experienced cameraman pointed out that, when things go into overdrive, the observer's mind reacts with boosts of adrenaline. This drug affects your sense of time, and things do seem to happen more slowly. So I began to deliberately run my shots longer than my immediate reactions suggested.

Film was heavy to carry and expensive to use – £25 was the cost to buy and process one minute of film to the stage where you could simply look at it. So we tried to be reasonable with our shooting ratios: the ideal was 40:1. In other words, you'd shoot 40 minutes of film in the camera and expect that to be edited down to one minute in your finished film. But tricky sequences could run up to 100:1.

As for how long it would take to actually film something, the old numbers still pretty much apply today. For a minute of finished programme on the screen, you'll need to spend on average about eight days in the field. So an ambitious, pure-wildlife series, comprising 10 programmes, each 50 minutes long, will have 10 x 50 x 8, ie, 4000 filming days in its budget. That's why they don't come cheap.

Communication, on the other hand, has changed utterly. When I first worked in the Antarctic 36 years ago, everything was by telex. We were allowed to send 200 words of personal traffic each month and could receive 100. Now the film crew can talk to the office by satellite phone as often as they want, and can even send images.

Maybe it's a throwback to my BAS days, but I'm much more inclined to adopt the principle of 'no news is good news'. In other words, if you don't hear from me, assume all's going OK. I like giving big environments and animals my total concentration. I prefer to sink into the subtleties of their moods so that maybe, just maybe, I can find the advantage that shows in the pictures I bring back. I like as few distractions as possible. And if that includes the office, well fine by me.

Many places are now, of course, much less arduous to reach, and there's a lot more knowledge and experience about some locations today. I'm thinking of the underwater life of the Red Sea, for example, or the game parks in Africa. The best example is the Antarctic continent itself. In 1976, on my first trip south, only one tour ship and a few private yachts visited the Peninsula. Now you can take your choice from any one of 20 tour companies. ■

Heavyweight. The housings for the first broadcast-quality tape cameras were heavy beasts to carry around topside – bigger and weightier than those for film cameras. But they were designed to be neutrally buoyant under water. So once you had them under the ice, swimming with them was no problem.

Curiosity. What's lovely about this image is that it's the whale who's come to look down at me. I've done the classic – quietly snorkelled deep and made myself an object of curiosity – and so she's swum across to check me out. Her six-week-old baby calf above is less confident.

Companionship. Some humpbacks clearly became very accustomed to the sound of our boat. This one even seemed to like it, parking himself under our hull for an hour one afternoon.

In the Company of Whales

I've spent many weeks filming humpbacks in the Antarctic during the summer. But the murky, plankton-green water off the Peninsula doesn't let you see them under water in all their glory. For that experience you must travel to the blue coral seas off Tonga, where the females go to give birth.

The most vivid impression anyone has of whales is their size. That sounds obvious – they're the biggest animals on the planet, aren't they? But they do truly take on whole new dimensions when you experience them under water. Seeing them from a boat, you catch a brief glimpse of perhaps a fin and part of a back breaking the surface – if you're very lucky, perhaps a spyhopping head. But under water, the whole animal is in gentle motion before you.

When approached in the right way, 18 metres of curious mammal will hang in the water, and a good swimmer can often ease in close. 'Good' here means having an almost indefinable affinity with the animal and the sea. It's not just how you physically move in the water, it's what's going on in your head as well. 'Good' thoughts involve respect, fascination, a willingness to be friendly – if you offer all these, then the whale will reciprocate, until finally you're eye to eye and do indeed have a relationship.

Sue and I spent ten weeks in Tonga filming humpbacks with their calves for *Planet Earth*. In that time we had magical encounters with whales. Lole, our boat skipper, was a man in a million, a native Tongan who had been on the water all his life. He never rushed, he was never flustered. I'd only met one other man in my life who could handle a boat around whales like Lole could.*

Lole taught me that the first time in the water in the company of a whale, I should swim very slowly, and if I was lucky enough to see the whale, be content to keep my distance. "She'll know you're there as soon as you slip into the water," he said. "So give her plenty of time to grow accustomed to you. Stay at the limit of visibility, don't crowd her. Give her a chance to get to know you." It was wise advice. With some whales it might take an afternoon of quiet following before I felt confident about going close enough to see them clearly. And even then, some were obviously more relaxed with me than others. Over time, we came to recognise the friendliest ones. 'String Tail' had been injured at some time in her life; she had strips of skin hanging off one tip of her tail flukes. She was never laid back. So when we saw her, we didn't even bother to try to film her. On the other hand, there was another female with a white patch on her tail that looked like a flying bird. She was easy.

Initially, when the calves were only a few days or weeks old, the whales were difficult to approach. The mums were very protective, always turning away and keeping themselves between us and the calves. But as the calves grew, the mums became more tolerant. If a calf was curious about us, its mum would be less bothered. It was then we had the best encounters.

▶

Hydrodynamics. Look at this humpback's long pectoral flippers. Their scalloped leading edges have been shown to be more efficient at sweeping through the water than they would be if they were simply straight. Engineers are now looking at designing similarly shaped wind-turbine blades.

Eye to eye. When a whale is swimming horizontally, it can see things most easily that are directly below it. The vertebrae in its neck are also fused, and so it can't move its head like we can. These two facts explain why the female is vertical in the water: she's taken up the best position for watching me.

Lumpy heads. Up close, you can clearly see the ping-pong-sized knobbles on the heads of the humpbacks. These are hair follicles, each with a single coarse hair. No one is quite sure of their purpose, but it's probably sensory.

▶ One day I was filming a calf while Sue was filming me. We were about 20 metres apart when the calf decided to take a closer look at Sue. She had the wide-angle on the lens and kept filming as the calf swam towards her. But then for some reason the young whale thought to look back at me. A whale can't turn its head – the bones in its neck are fused together and so it has to turn its whole body. As the calf twisted to glance at me, it swept its tail to make the turn and accidentally swiped Sue's ankle.

As Sue described it later, she felt like she'd "been hit by a sledgehammer". She screamed in pain and dropped the camera, which started going glug glug down into the depths. I was 20 metres away and had seen the whole thing. I was now faced with a choice. Save Sue? Or save the camera? No points for the right answer.

Sue was in pain, but floating. The camera, with her great shots on the tape, was disappearing. Only one course of action – it took me maybe about 15 seconds to dive down to retrieve the camera. It took Sue only about five years to forgive me.

*In case you're wondering who could handle a boat around whales like Lole, it's Jerome Poncet, skipper of the *Golden Fleece*, with whom I sailed many times to the Antarctic.

Tonga, South Pacific, September, filming for *Planet Earth*, BBC.

Mean machine. The producer Frances Berrigan and I checked out the army trucks we were going to use to take all our gear onto the lake. Good job that the ice was more than a metre thick.

The Baikal Circus

Misch's motorbike was the strangest form of transport I've ever used. But if sitting with my camera in the sidecar wasn't odd enough, there was also the complete novelty of rattling at 60kph over ice so smooth and clear it was almost transparent, over water more than 1500 metres deep, while I looked for a unique species of seal in central Siberia more than 2000 kilometres from the nearest ocean. Locations don't come any weirder than Lake Baikal in winter.

As we prepared the camping equipment, I could see this was going to be a shoot like no other. No small snow machines for this crew. We had full-blown caterpillar-tracked army trucks full of people, food for three weeks, an enormous canvas tent, and many, many tree trunks.

The crew opened the vodka. We dipped our fingers in our glasses, sprinkled a few drops onto the ice to gain the favour of the Baikal spirits, then rolled out onto the frozen lake.

A couple of hours later, we set up camp. It was like a circus come to town. The tent was shaped exactly like a big top. I realised why they'd brought all the wood when they used it to build a large raised platform round the inside of the tent. Mattresses on top made a big communal sleeping area. I thought at first it was up off the ice for warmth, but then they assembled a wood-burning stove in the middle. For the week we were there, that stove was always burning.

The surface of the ice quickly melted, and we sloshed around in a few centimetres of water the whole time – our feet at zero degrees, our heads up in temperatures that wouldn't disgrace a sauna.

The freshwater ice itself was completely transparent. Inside the tent it was like living on one of those disco floors lit from below. An eerie blue glow illuminated everything. The guys drilled a hole in one corner and dropped a baited line through it. Under our feet, we could watch fish swimming that a few minutes later might be caught, gutted and in the pot.

The Baikal seal is a close relative of the ringed seal. Scientists speculate that 1–2 million years ago, an ice age meant that the shores of the Arctic Ocean were much closer than today. Ringed seals swam up the short river that linked that sea to Lake Baikal. When the ice retreated, they were stranded in the lake and have remained there ever since.

Though there are no polar bears within 2000 kilometres of Baikal, the seals haven't lost any of the ringed's wariness and are very difficult to approach. The only success I had was by using Misch's little hunting sledge with the white sail on it (see page 48). On my knees, crouching down behind, pushing it in front of me, I could sometimes slide close enough to film them. The secret was for me to move only when the seal was having one of its 20-second, head-down, micro-sleep periods. The moment it lifted its head to look around, I froze immobile.

Baikal has been isolated for millions of years, and so evolution has taken many strange pathways: 70 per cent of the species living in it are found nowhere else on Earth. In one place, I dived among metre-high fingers of green sponges that were hundreds of years old, while filming ▶

Wallace and Gromit – Soviet style. Misch's trusty
350cc IZH motorbike and sidecar were the best way
to travel around on the frozen lake surface.

Slide-hide. The seals on Lake Baikal were so wary that I ended up using this modified sledge. Crouched behind the white sail, I could move in close enough to film.

▶ bright red spiny amphipods crawling around on the lake bed.

Lake Baikal in 1988 offered a last chance to visit the old-style Soviet Union. The trip would have been impossible a few years earlier because of Cold War politics, and impractical a few years later in the chaos that followed the full implementation of perestroika and glasnost. But we experienced the very best of what didn't change: the trust and hospitality of our local guides and assistants.

After finishing filming, on the afternoon before we were due to fly out, we were taken for a picnic in the woods a few miles from the village. With the cameras packed away, I could chill out on the local delicacy: mushrooms well pickled in vodka.

I remember nothing beyond five o'clock, when Misch and I were putting the increasingly blurred world to rights. I woke 13 hours later in the thin light of early dawn, in an unknown bed. Stumbling outside, I recognised no landmarks. The small shop farther down the road and the signposts at the junctions were, of course, in Russian and so utterly unintelligible. I had no idea where I was, and we were flying out in four hours.

I had two options – worry about what might happen or go back to bed on the assumption that whoever carried me there would also come to collect me. Sure enough, a couple of hours later, the producer was shaking me awake, saying it was time to go.

Lake Baikal, Siberia, Russia, March, filming for *Baikal – Blue Eye of Siberia,* Cicada Films.

Right
Haul-out. This young Baikal seal is pulling itself out of its breathing hole onto the top of the ice. You can see the big strong claws on the flippers, which it uses to keep breathing holes open in winter.

Below left
Chill-out. In summer, Baikal seals haul out on the rocks to bask in the sun. They're still wary as hell. I had to hide behind trees on the shore of one of the Ushkanyi Islands to take this shot.

Below right
Antiquarian sponges. I'd never seen anywhere like Baikal under water. These fingers of sponge are hundreds of years old. The lake was granted World Heritage Site status in 1996 because of its unique flora and fauna.

Murky Waters

Ethics is a subject that can have the film-makers themselves at each other's throats. How should we behave around animals? How much respect should we give our viewers when it comes to the final programme?

I reckon there are two cardinal rules we should all follow when filming wildlife. First, the welfare of our subjects must be paramount. Second, we must never deceive our audience. Simple and acceptable to all, surely?

Yes, of course. But let's think about that. Consider these questions, beloved by one producer. Where would you stop in the following series? Would you deliberately feed a fly to a spider? A stickleback to a pike? A rabbit to a fox? A baby rabbit to a fox? A penguin to a leopard seal? An antelope to a lion? A man to a crocodile?

The last step is of course inconceivable (though the devil in me is always tempted to ask, "Which man in particular are we considering?"), but it's revealing to decide where you stand on the way up to there.

Hold to some religious faiths, and you wouldn't even accept the first, but in practical terms, that would rule out a great deal of filming of the very smallest subjects or add impossibly to the duration of a filming trip. Why do we feel less for a creepy-crawly than for mammals? Tough calls.

I'd say there are times and places when 'manipulation' is necessary and acceptable, though for me, only well down the scale. That point at which moral discomfort becomes unacceptable is hugely, personally variable. It depends on the individual, his or her own ambitions, culture and sensitivity to the situation, which animals are involved in the sequence and what behaviour is wanted. But what happens when the director wants a shot that requires doing something that the cameraperson thinks unreasonable? Does position in the chain of command give a person more or less right to decide?

Often the issue can be one of not just moral sensitivity but actual knowledge of the animal. Too many of those involved in wildlife film-making, and especially, dare I say, those higher up the commissioning chain – the executives for whom the viewing figures are paramount – simply don't know enough about the animal to make a judgement on what's reasonable to expect from the production team in the field. The message from the high levels, albeit subliminally, is all about bringing back the big sequence. I believe that if we had leadership in morality coming from them, low-quality tooth-and-claw television wouldn't be as popular as it is now.

For me, the question of non-disturbance, the idea of being at one with my subject, is at the heart of why I mostly stick to genuinely wild situations and rarely film animals smaller than a rabbit. I have the greatest admiration for those who construct sets so lifelike that their subjects accept them and behave naturally in them. It's just that I like my animals so big that true nature is the only possible backdrop.

But even in those perfect circumstances, I make decisions all the time about what is and isn't possible, feasible or acceptable to try to film. Being too close to animals or following them for too long can cause them stress so that they swim or walk faster than they would do naturally. If they're with their youngsters or at another crucial life stage, when perhaps food is scarce, then that extra expenditure of their ▶

Approach with respect. Working close to whales without bothering them is possible with an experienced crew and the right tools. In this case, we had the *Golden Fleece* as our base, with Jerome driving, the filming inflatable powered by an electric motor rather than a noisy outboard, and the time and patience to spend a couple of hours on the water before finally we had the whales this close.

Treat with respect. It's all too easy to grant human characteristics to animals when they do something that looks human. This bear is clearly relaxed, but under his cuddly-looking furry exterior is a big, clever predator. Being chased by him might make a good story for the pub but it doesn't give you any meaningful behaviour for the film. I'd rather leave him relaxed.

▶ energy reserves while I'm with them may be crucial to their survival. Unwittingly, I the film-maker may jeopardise their chances if I don't know my animal well enough. It's possible that I'll simply try too hard.

But if I'm given enough time, that will improve my chances. For the big series, the rule of thumb is that a week in the field will produce a minute on the screen. That 60-minute show needs 420 filming days. I know such a long time makes programmes expensive, but don't expect consistent, new, ground-breaking wildlife material if you give your camera crews less.

How might we deceive our audience? Every time we make a decision on a camera setting, we affect how the picture is seen. A big telephoto lens offers details way better than our eyes, and slow-motion will let us see the behaviour much more clearly than in real time. But slowing down the frame rate also makes animals look bigger on the screen. Fair enough for every shot of the majestic eagle, star of our show?

In 1995 we wanted to do a sequence that had never been filmed before – of newly born polar bear cubs in their den. We were advised by the best polar bear researchers that even to attempt to put a camera into a real den would likely result in such disturbance that the mother bear would abandon the den and leave any cubs to die.

So our solution was to build a false den on the side of a Belgian zoo cage where there was a pregnant female bear. The 'den' interior was in total darkness, but we illuminated it with infrared light, invisible to the bear but filmable with special cameras that we mounted outside little viewing windows in the walls. Using these we managed great shots of the very small cubs when they were only a few centimetres long.   ▶

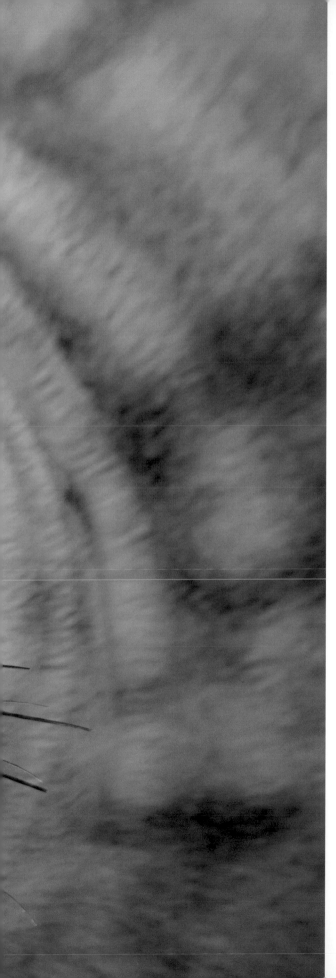

Keep your distance. A Weddell can sleep soundly because there are no polar bears in the Antarctic. It may be the most placid of the southern seals, but that doesn't mean it won't be stressed if you're too close. So a long lens is what's needed for a close-up if you want natural behaviour.

▶ However, in the final narration, we didn't make it clear that this was not in fact a real den. The press got hold of this, and we were vilified for deception. But for me and the producer, Martha Holmes, it was we who held the moral high ground. We'd used the knowledge of the scientists, the skill of model-makers and the dedication of a team of camerapersons to monitor our den round the clock for a week to gain a minute of unique footage. To have tried to do it any other way would have endangered the lives of the bears.

Should we have told the viewers either before the show or during it that these scenes were 'staged'? Perhaps, but then we'd probably have had just as many complaining that such information detracted from their viewing experience. The BBC's *Frozen Planet* series came in for the same criticism (albeit from a tiny minority of the press) for showing tiny cubs in a den filmed using similar techniques. Proof that this is a place for shades of opinion, where there's no pleasing everyone but where surely the important factor is that no risk was posed to the polar bears.

I think it's insightful to see how camerapeople and directors respond to the question, "What's the most dangerous thing you've ever filmed?" It can often be interpreted as "How close did you get to your subject?" Some people seek a buzz by being up close and intimate with whatever they're filming. There's nothing wrong with that per se, as long as it doesn't stress the animal or you're not doing it for some cheap thrill that you or the viewer will experience.

While some animals and situations are, for sure, potentially hazardous, 'dangerous' is a very emotive and subjective term. What appears risky to some people is less so if you're accustomed to the conditions. And while a charge or attack by an animal might be a good story to tell ▶

▶ afterwards, it won't make the final cut in a movie about natural behaviour. I'm here now, with this great behaviour happening in front of me, because of the efforts of a big team behind me. I don't want to screw it up by going too close and either frightening the animal away or having it take more interest in me than in carrying on with the behaviour I want to film. The filming of natural behaviour would always come first for me in that situation.

Ethics doesn't stop when you've filmed the sequence. The old journalist's maxim of never allowing the facts to get in the way of a good story is as relevant at the edit as it ever was for the printed page. The purist could argue that the second the first editorial cut is made, we're imposing our version of what happened on what was genuine reality. But showing behaviour uncut at full duration is clearly a non-starter: it would last far too long on the screen. A lion chasing, killing and eating, or a penguin coming back to its youngster to feed it is almost always going to be an amalgamation of several chases and several penguin returnings. What the viewer will see is an idealised sequence. But as long as it shows what could happen in reality, I'm fine with the process.

What I don't accept are misleading biological 'facts' paraded out in the commentary to heighten the drama or bring that part of the programme to a neat end. Granting animals human-like emotions or motives is fine with some species but not with others.

I always feel the animals are fascinating enough without making up details about their true nature, and to do otherwise is effectively to disrespect your subject – and also to woefully underestimate the intelligence of whoever's watching. ■

Don't crowd them. These almost-fledged Adélie chicks are straining to get what could be their last meal. The parent has just led them on a 'food chase' – a runaround as part of their natural behaviour to build up their stamina. If food is in short supply, only the stronger one will get fed. The last thing they need now is a cameraperson too close so they're disturbed and can't be fed properly.

FREEZE FRAME

POLAR HEAVEN

Previous page
Summer sunset at the Fish Islands,
Antarctic Peninsula.

Stardust Fireflies

Halley Research Station is based where it is for one principal reason – the study of upper atmospheric phenomena such as the aurora australis. I'd never seen an aurora before I spent my year there in 1983, but over that winter, we had several memorable displays. There were 100 days from early May until early August when the sun was permanently below the horizon, and on weekends especially we kept an aurora watch.

Someone would go out every hour or so just to see what was developing. It might begin as a quiet green arc off in the distance but then could swirl to directly overhead. Great curtains of flickering light moved sinuously across the whole width of the sky, the rays dancing down at times like individual searchlights, at other times all vaguely diffuse, with only the very lowest edge having any definition. It should have been accompanied by some vast dramatic noise, but somehow the utter silence made it all the more impressive. It was the scale that blew me away – this was all happening 300 kilometres or more above my head, and at times it filled the whole sky.

I loved the terms that the ionospheric scientists used to explain the aurora. Normally dry and close to unintelligible, geek-speak became poetry when they referred to the solar wind as being like an ocean current in space, carrying energised particles at almost the speed of light away from the sun. This wind strikes the gases in our high, thin atmosphere, exciting the individual gas molecules to even higher levels. As they drop back to their ground state, they lose that extra energy by giving off light, which we saw as the aurora.

When we had an aurora party at 35 degrees below zero, with hot gluhwein, it only took half a dozen drinks before I was having the vision of the aurora overhead as the life and death of countless billions of stardust fireflies.

We experimented with camera settings while we tried to take photographs that would convey the spectacle. In the days before digital there was no instant feedback of what you'd just taken. I remember that, for aurora photography, you started with all the 2s – f2 for 20 seconds with 200 ISO film.

British Antarctic Survey Research Station, Halley, Brunt Ice Shelf, Weddell Sea, Antarctica, June.

Sundog and Diamond Dust

If you're out when it's thinly overcast, put a hand up to shield the very brightest part of the sun and then look at the sky at an angle of about 22 degrees from your hand. You may well pick out a faint ring against the clouds. That's the same effect you're witnessing as this one here, though mine is probably way more spectacular than anything you'll see. Not that I'm competitive, you understand.

We'd seen them before but never so bright as on that Sunday morning, nor so ideally placed just over base. This was a sundog, or parhelion, to give it its proper meteorological term. While we watched, tiny hexagonal platelets of ice drifted down from the sky to settle briefly on our clothes. It was these platelets that were causing the phenomenon as sunlight refracted through them. When they fall randomly, a complete circle of bright light appears around the sun. But if they drop vertically, then the light waves are all bent horizontally, creating the hot spots of the sundog.

The ice crystals are so small and they fall so slowly that you see them as tiny motes of flashing light called diamond dust – surely the most poetic of meteorological terms.

When I followed references to parhelion on the web, I discovered how historians reported that on the morning of the Battle of Mortimer's Cross in England in 1461, 'three suns' appeared. The effect utterly frightened the troops until their commander convinced them that it represented the Holy Trinity, and thus God was on their side. Clearly it was a parhelion they were witnessing. So I now look at this picture and imagine the Yorkist troops marching to their ideal battle song – David Bowie's 'Diamond Dogs'.

British Antarctic Survey Research Station, Signy Island, South Orkney Islands, Antarctica, August.

The Spinning Sky

One of the regular duties on Signy was nightwatch. Every person took turns, a week at a time. You had to be up between midnight and eight, doing fire safety checks around the base every hour, keeping an eye on the generators, baking bread for breakfast and, just before dawn, changing the sunshine card.

The ingeniously simple sunshine recorder consisted of a glass ball on a tiny pedestal. Curving around parallel to the ball but separated from it by a gap maybe 5cm wide was a metal band with a broad groove in it. A strip of Met Office standardised paper-card slotted into the groove, and as the sun's rays passed through the globe, they were focused onto the card and burnt a hole in it.

Brief sunny spells just produced spots of black, but full sun for an hour burnt a continuous line. Take away the card at the end of every day and you had an accurate measure of when and for how long the sun had been shining.

I was up there doing the card when a magnificent midsummer sunrise developed. There was no sea ice, and the wind was strong and bitterly cold from the north, stacking up a massive lenticular cloud over Coronation Island. The scene had a power and scale that was positively breathtaking, and I felt it all the more acutely since I was the only one witnessing it. The scene lasted maybe ten minutes before the sun rose, the orange faded and the cloud lost its spin.

Coronation Island, South Orkney Islands, Antarctica, January.

Crystal Clouds

Clouds you rarely see in the sky at home are almost commonplace at the poles. But that doesn't mean they lose any of their wonder.

I saw this iridescent cloud from the lounge window one August afternoon. Any day on Signy when you caught a glimpse of blue sky was worth celebrating, and so this was definitely a moment for a picture.

White light is what we see when all seven of the principal visible colours are mixed together. The classic unmixed image is the one showing those spectral colours radiating from the glass prism – think *Dark Side of the Moon* album cover. The distinct rays splinter out at discrete angles because each colour has its own wavelength. So it's bent or diffracted to a different degree when it passes from air into the glass and then back into the air again. Substitute the glass prism with tiny, uniformly shaped ice crystals high in the polar clouds, and you will see exactly the same rainbow-coloured iridescent effect I saw here above Jane Peak.

Signy Island, South Orkney Islands, Antarctica, September.

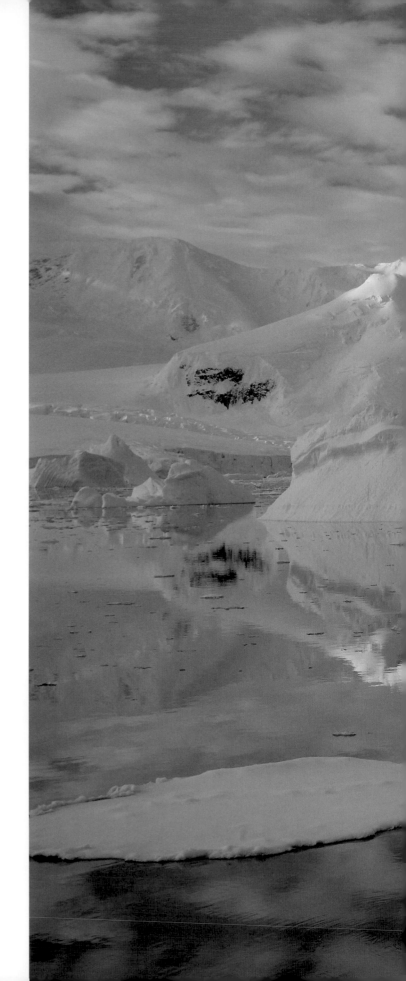

Loneliness, All the Blues and Kate Bush

I'm often asked, "What did you miss the most when you spent those long times away with the British Antarctic Survey?" And depending on my mood, I reply that sometimes there was a real ache to see family and friends – though to be honest, that feeling never lasted too long. The perfect fantasy break was a long weekend – going back home Friday night and then heading south again on the following Tuesday. Just enough time for a good catch-up.

Occasionally the routine of base would bear down on me, especially if we were suffering a four- or five-day blow, when white-out prevailed and it just wasn't worth going out. And yes, of course, the complete lack of women drove us to distraction – at times.

Two things I did miss, especially in winter, were smell and colour. At low temperatures, smells just don't have the chance to be created. The penguin rookery in full summer made your eyes stream from the pungent ammonia stink of Adélie faeces, but in midwinter the mud was hard as iron and didn't smell of anything. All those stinking summer molecules that assailed your nostrils were just frozen solid to the ground. As for colours, I missed especially greens and reds. Some days were just all shades of blue.

But even that could hold a special loveliness if muted cloud cover and flat calm prevailed. This picture is one of my favourites. It oozes tranquillity but also brings to mind a much-played track from an album we had on base: Kate Bush singing about her 'Symphony in Blue' from *Lionheart*. Listening to that and gazing at Kate on the cover didn't help take your mind off women, though.

Dallmann Bay, Antarctic Peninsula, February, filming for *Life*, BBC.

ICE, SNOW,
COLD AND COLDER

Me – Warm and Comfortable

I put this picture [previous page] on the screen in presentations because everyone then thinks how rugged and tough a man I must be. When I go on to tell my audience how at times my eyelashes froze together, another wave of involuntary shivering passes through the rows.

But if truth be known, I was actually quite comfortable when I asked Jason to take this shot. The air was cold, about -30°C, but I had been walking fast and breathing hard in almost nil wind, with my hood pulled well up. The windproof material of the anorak has thin, semi-flexible wire sewn into the opening of the hood. When you bend this, it forms a tunnel in front of your face, preventing windchill reaching your exposed skin. In fact, it's so calm in the tunnel that exhaled air full of moisture hangs around your face, freezing again on your eyelashes and clothing. These are the 'gombles', much sought after by those who wish to lay claim to being polar heroes.

There are times, however, when staying warm is crucial. And maybe my secret weapon comes from having spent so much time working down south for the British Antarctic Survey before I ever had to be creative and use a camera in extreme conditions.

In my winters with BAS, I learned to walk the narrow line between being chilled and being frostbitten. I'm aware now of the momentary tingling that precedes frost-nip damage. When I feel that, I don't ignore it. I make sure my hands and feet get some heat. Everyone has a weak spot, and once that's chilled, the rest of the body loses it. For me it's my head. I have to wear a hat even at temperatures hovering around zero. If I don't, I quickly become chilled all over.

At the end of the day, however, discomfort of some kind comes with the wildlife-filming territory. Who's suffering more, me with numbing fingers and toes or my fellow cameraperson being eaten alive by mosquitoes in that hide in the rainforest?

Kong Karl's Land, Svalbard, March, filming for Planet Earth, BBC.

Fun with Footprints

The conditions for creating raised footsteps are quite simple but very specific. You need a 15cm fall of fresh, light snow in windless conditions at about -12°C. Someone then goes for a walk over the brow of the hill, taking big strides through the virgin snow. The person comes back on almost the same route.

An hour later the wind picks up, and for the rest of the day it's 30 knots, sufficient to blow away all the powder – except from the tracks themselves. The compressed snow of the footprints froze shortly after they were made. Now, like reversed Yeti prints, they stand proud of the snow.

Signy Island, South Orkney Islands, Antarctica, September.

Anything for a Shot

It's the wind on top of the cold that's the killer at the poles. Windchill is exactly that, the super-fast cooling of faces and hands as the breeze picks up. Wind sucks away heat from exposed flesh at a fearsome pace – 30 knots at -30°C really can freeze your skin in seconds.

I was coming back from a chilly afternoon filming Weddell seals on the west coast. The shoot hadn't been very successful, and the sky had been overcast for most of the time. But as I trudged over the pass separating one side of the island from the other, my head tucked down out of the strengthening bitter wind, the clouds cleared. The sun was still just above the hills, and I was aware of a river of backlit drifting snow streaming past at ankle height over the edge of the slope. It's moments like this when a bit of you really wishes you weren't quite so photographically obsessed – how much warmer you'd stay with hands in gloves, just looking. But the god of Kodak could not be ignored. I dug the camera out of my pack and took this shot.

Jane Col, Signy Island, South Orkney Islands, Antarctica, August.

A Good Place to Sleep

We found this monster crevasse halfway up Huayna Potosi in Bolivia. We were trying to carry as little equipment as possible on our so-called Alpine-style ascent. But this meant sleeping bags in the open air – not the best idea in the rainy season – hoping it wouldn't snow. This big hole, on the other hand, looked well protected, and we decided to risk any falling icicles in return for a dry place for the night.

    After admiring the massive stalactite ice spears in the roof, we wondered long and hard about the formation of the curved icicles we found at the bottom of the hole. The most tenable theory we came up with was that winds must occasionally gust even down there, strong enough for the drops of water at the tips of the icicles to be blown to the side or upwards. So the direction of the icicles' growth depends effectively on the strength of the storms on the slopes.

Cordillera Real, Bolivia, April, on a mountaineering expedition.

Flowers of the Ice Fields

Beautifully delicate 'frost flowers' grow scattered across the surface of newly formed sea ice or where water has flooded out over the ice. Flooding can happen when the tide rises and the ice floating on top becomes jammed against the shore. The ice then can't rise any more, and so the water comes through the cracks and forms pools on top. These pools then freeze.

When the temperature is very low, around -25°C or so, and it's flat calm above, an entire bay can freeze solid overnight. The whole surface then twinkles with tiny, fragile, three-dimensional crystals. They never last longer than a couple of days or so, because as soon as the ice thickens, they stop growing.

But for those few days, if you're out with a snow machine, the flowers can be a valuable clue to dangerously thin patches on the frozen sea. Greyish ice is the normal give-away, a sure sign of new ice, but if the sun is glinting off a field of frost flowers ahead, then it's also worth avoiding the area, or at least giving your snow machine plenty of throttle so that you zoom over at full speed.

Borge Bay, Signy Island, South Orkney Islands, Antarctica, July.

Sticky Porridge to Smooth Pancakes

Perhaps it's a sign of how hungry the first polar explorers were, but many of the terms that they used for the stages of sea ice are named after food.

The freezing point of normal salinity seawater is -1.7°C, and the transformation to ice happens in the calm, cold days of autumn. It's quite different from the freezing of fresh water.

With the air temperature around -15°C or so, a thin layer of grease ice appears as a slick on the surface of the cold sea. Over a few hours this can thicken to porridge ice, a slushy slurry of ice crystals that still moves with the swell but in a heavier sort of way. It's very sticky and can be a real drag on a small ship's hull that's trying to push through patches of it. If the temperature stays low and the swell still jostles the ice, the porridge thickens further and small floes develop. This is pancake ice, the edges of the floes being gently pushed up as the ice lumps bump together.

In time, the pancakes freeze together until you have what every film-maker wants – sea ice solid enough to drive out on and look for your subjects.

North Point, Signy Island, South Orkney Islands, Antarctica, April.

The Ice That Came to Life

I walked past this piece of ice every day for a couple of weeks after it washed up on some shallow flats on a very high spring tide. To be honest, it didn't impress me much. I hardly gave it a glance – rounded, no remarkable silhouette to it, just typically weathered faces with little dimples on them, caused simply by gentle wave action over the time it had been floating in the water.

Then early one morning, returning from a Weddell seal count on the west coast, I saw it in a different light. The sun was clear on the horizon, unusual for Signy, where manky clag and overcast was the norm. I was drawn to the berg, which was now shining like a jewel, practically transparent.

It was an odd sort of light, for though the sun was still low, it had none of the orange you'd usually associate with the first hour after dawn. It was bright, brilliant and blue. And it gave me a picture that may be simple but to me is full of the magically variable beauty of ice.

Shallow Bay, Signy Island, South Orkney Islands, Antarctica, May.

The Berg That Turned

Icebergs symbolise the polar seas, and I never tire of the shapes and colours they display. They're especially lovely when they decay sufficiently for a big chunk to fall off, through the berg either melting or simply breaking apart. Then the centre of buoyancy of the berg suddenly changes. It will roll over a little and maybe even turn turtle, exposing surfaces to the air that have been weathered under water for weeks, months or even years.

I often saw grooves like this in the sides of bergs, and I thought they were caused by rain or meltwater – until a glaciologist told me the true reason.

Snow that's fallen on top of a glacier is slowly turned to ice under the weight of more snow accumulating on top. In that ice, tiny air bubbles are trapped and compressed. This berg was once floating almost level with the sea surface, but as it melted in the slightly warmer waters of summer, those tiny bubbles were gradually released one by one. Where there were overhangs, bubbles followed their predecessors up the same lines, creating grooves in the ice. They cut them deeper where the ice was fractionally less dense but barely created an impression in the areas where the ice was hardest.

All this took place out of sight under water, until one day the berg broke, and the physics of buoyancy were then revealed in this uniquely artistic piece of natural sculpture.

Port Charcot, Antarctic Peninsula, January, filming for *The Blue Planet*, BBC.

Cliff Face

Halley Research Station is so isolated that only one ship a year brings in new supplies and scientists. The relief vessel ties up not to a rocky shore but alongside the ice cliffs of the Brunt Ice Shelf. Like the leading edge of a glacier, these cliffs are constantly changing their profile as bergs break away or smaller pieces of ice drop off into the sea.

I was on the ship when the arrival of heavy pack ice, driven by the wind and currents, temporarily forced her off its moorings. For 24 hours we'd been dodging the biggest of the floes, but the worst had passed. The sea was free of ice again. It was as the ship was slowly easing back into position that I suddenly noticed this face in the cornice of the ice cliff. I just had time to run to my cabin, grab a camera and take one picture before the perspective altered and it disappeared. I don't think anyone else on board saw it.

Cliffs of the Brunt Ice Shelf, Weddell Sea, Antarctica, December.

Glacial Rapids

You might think of ice as a solid, but it's much better imagined as a very viscous plastic that slides downwards slowly but inexorably. You'll never see this better than when flying over some high polar ice cap, where the ice feeds glaciers that then flow down to the sea through mountain valleys. Squeezed between the sides of the valley as it is on the right in this picture, the glacier surface is smooth and unbroken. But as it comes clear of the mountains, the river of ice is suddenly freed from any restrictions. It changes mood from constrained to chaotic, the surface riven by huge transverse cracks. It's impossible to cross by any means.

In the centre of the shot, beyond the glacier's crevasses, where the snow slopes climb to meet the rocks of the mountain, are just the sort of places where you find polar bear dens. I spent one March on Svalbard hoping to film a den emergence, checking for dens by driving along the sea ice and scanning the slopes with binoculars. But that became impossible when the ice broke out unseasonally early.

The only alternative was to explore the land near the shore by driving down the glaciers from the inland ice. But no chance over a glacier like this one. I came home empty-handed from that shoot.

Svalbard, Arctic, filming for *Ultimate Killers*, BBC.

Descending. The linesman is clearly visible up above, while
Rick, my buddy, is also attached to the safety line.

Eye Beneath the Ice

Were you ever to dive beneath the ice as we did on Signy, this is what
you'd see coming back to the hole. You might be bored by that stage
if the dive had been some tedious, sedentary sampling experiment,
or completely the opposite if you'd been down filming Weddell seals.
You might be so cold you'd forgotten what your feet felt like, or still
pleasantly warm if you'd had enough tea pre-dive to be able to pee in
your wetsuit a few times.

But either way, I always got a buzz from looking back up through
the hole to the man holding the safety line. We pretty much always
used a line, and if handled correctly, you hardly noticed it was there.

"Imagine I'm a fish on it," I'd say. "Don't tug at me, just hold the rope
tight enough to feel me on the end."

The second diver would be on a sliding buddy, a shorter length of
line with a carabiner on each end. One end was attached to the diver,
the other to the main safety tether, so that the second diver could slide
up and down the line but still be attached to it. An apple float halfway
along the buddy line kept it up off the bottom – a simple system, but
it worked.

Nothing can prepare you for diving under ice in winter. Icebergs
are pushed inshore by the tides and wind, settling on the bottom
where they might be stuck for months. Though the sea freezes around

them, the sea ice is always cracked right in close to the berg where
the ice moves up and down with the tide. In places, these cracks are
alternative access points for us to go exploring under water.

Slanting sunbeams pierce the gloom, shining through the cracks in
the ice above – sharp-edged, white light-sabres, growing impossibly
narrow as they lance into the depths. It is edgily claustrophobic, yet
with a simultaneous sensation of huge, blue space all around.

Under flat ice, the visibility can exceed 60 metres horizontally. But
if there is heavy snow cover on top, the place has the gloominess of
a barely lit room. In other areas, where the ice floes have been driven
together by the wind or currents, the ice forms a pressure ridge. Broken
pieces of floe are jumbled five metres high above the water and five
times as deep below. A good rule is if that if it is chaotic on top, it's a
challengingly interesting icescape below.

Swimming in the caverns of ice, you see the brightly lit cracks and
the different colours of ice where it varies in thickness. Then you realise
how many visual cues a seal has as it navigates its way back to its
breathing hole.

If we adjusted for neutral buoyancy, no swimming would be
required and we could be motionless in the water, listening. Had we
left the surface when the wind was blowing, with snow scurrying ▶

Squeezing through. Clear visibility but gloomy low light.
Diving under ice near bergs isn't for the claustrophobic.

Icefish. Normally, this fish prefers to lie on the bottom.
So you have to be quick to get under one for a shot
from this angle.

▶ across the ice and all seeming very hostile, under the ice could truly feel like another world, a haven of peace.

On some dives we'd see curious icicles like stalactites under the ice. They were very fragile, made up of tiny platelets of ice fused together and forming a hollow tube. What happens is that, as the sea ice forms, there's a gradation in the salinity between the top of the ice and the bottom. A layer of water that's super-salty builds up at the lower surface. More salt makes this layer more dense, with a lower freezing point than normal, and just as water drips off the roof of a cave, so this hyper-saline brine drips into the seawater. But these salty droplets are super-cooled, so that normal seawater freezes when it comes into contact with them. It's these frozen platelets that form the tubular icicle. When conditions were right, you could clearly see the super-saline brine flowing out of the tube, producing a lime-juice effect in the water due to its different density.

Antarctica is a remarkably colourful place under water, rich with invertebrates found nowhere else. The best sites are under the overhangs where the rock faces aren't scoured by the icebergs that trundle into the bay every winter. Pink soft corals dangle down, orange anemones open their tentacles and the seaweed fronds carry *Antarcturus* isopods clinging to them.

We were often asked to send various live marine specimens from Signy back to the British Antarctic Survey (BAS) base in Cambridge. Icefish were popular – they looked weird for showing to the public,

and they were also fascinating biologically. An icefish appears white because it has no red-pigmented, oxygen-carrying haemoglobin in its blood. The cold waters of the Antarctic are rich enough in oxygen for the gas simply to diffuse directly through the fish's very thin skin into the tissues and blood vessels themselves.

Circulating in the icefish's blood vessels is another key to survival. Put a normal fish into Antarctic water and the -1.8°C temperature will turn its blood to a slush of ice crystals in matter of minutes. But icefish blood contains an antifreeze remarkably similar in chemistry to the stuff you pour into your car radiator. This means its blood stays fluid even at very low temperatures.

But on top of all that, ugly icefish held a special place in my heart. I owe them a personal debt of gratitude. When David Attenborough visited the Antarctic in 1981, while making *The Living Planet*, he had icefish on the list of animals to film. He and his crew called in at Signy for a few days, and I had the chance to help them with topside and underwater sequences. Icefish were the stars, and I knew just how to put them in front of the lens. The days I spent helping David and the film crew were when I first realised that these good people were doing something worthwhile, exciting and fascinating. They gave me the encouragement to go and try a movie camera myself.

Ten years later, I was working with them all for *Life in the Freezer*.

BAS Research Station, Signy Island, South Orkney Islands, Antarctica, winter.

The rewards of ice diving. Strands of the soft coral *Primnoella* hang down from the rock face, surrounded by splashes of colour from sponges and bryozoans. Underwater life here is as diverse as on any coral reef, though without the fish.

Right
Anemone feeding. Animals such as this are found only in well-protected places, where there is shelter from the scouring effect of the ice.

Far right
Isopod giant. If it lived in temperate waters, this *Antarcturus* crustacean would be millimetres long. In the Antarctic, it grows to several centimetres.

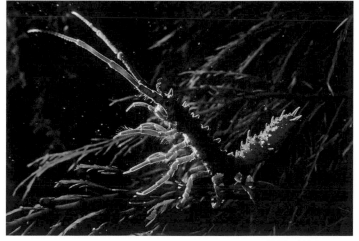

Crabbies, Ice and Fizz

Crabeater seals love ice. Like polar bears in the north, they'll stay on ice as long as there are floes big enough to carry them. Off the Antarctic Peninsula in summer, you'll often see small decaying pieces of iceberg or pack ice, each with its own wee crabbie population.

The water's usually murky with the last of the summer plankton bloom, the underwater portion of the ice glows green rather than blue, and the water temperature is around zero degrees. That means the small ice lumps are melting, and so the micro-bubbles of air trapped in the glacier ice of the bergy bit are released. These bubbles are so tiny that they take a long time to rise even the few feet to the surface, contributing to the general murkiness around the berg, where the water at times seems to be almost fizzing.

Antarctic Peninsula, February, filming for *Life*, BBC.

Close Encounters of the Crabeating Kind

Under the ice is a twilight world. Here the blue fades into black. Exhaled bubbles form silvery mirrors in the uneven ice roof, then run mercurially for escape through pale-veined tide cracks. The ice overhead damps down the ocean swell, and visibility in the still water seems limitless. It feels like being in a cathedral lit by suffused light from high windows and the doors closed for peace.

Rick and I hung in midwater, waiting for the crabeater seals. Though by far the most numerous of the five species of Antarctic seals, crabeaters are among the least accessible. They seldom venture close to shore, spending their lives among the heavy, drifting pack ice. Here on the island of Signy, in the northern Weddell Sea, they are a rarity.

We looked and listened but saw nothing as we finned slowly under the ice. Ahead, the mass of a berg seemed to glow with its own inner light. As we swam closer, the water-sculpted wall of ice became more distinct, its fluted vertical surfaces as smooth as polished marble but rippled as if a gently confused sea had suddenly turned to stone. There was a faint creaking, almost a crunching, as the berg moved with the current.

Crabeaters had appeared the night before – hundreds of dark bodies hauled out all along the sweeping 6 kilometres of ice edge. We had never seen them in such numbers and doubted if anyone had ever had such a chance to dive with them. Next morning, I was so excited that I hardly felt the slap of the freezing -1°C water against my lips as I stepped off the ice edge into the sea.

After ten minutes or so, almost subliminally, we heard the soft, low muttering of seals in the unseen distance. We were familiar with the deep grunts and long whistles of Weddell seals, but this crabeater sound was different, more broken and guttural, like old, heavy doors being opened slowly on un-oiled hinges. "Benevolent growling", as Rick described their voices later.

We glimpsed the crabbies first as shadows gliding round the lumps of pack ice at the limits of our vision, tail flippers lazily sideswiping. As if finding confidence in numbers, four or five swam straight towards us. Suddenly they had colour, texture and expression. Inquisitive faces peered at us only inches away. They nibbled tentatively at our air bubbles and sniffed at a proffered mitt. Silky bodies, pale tan with silvery flanks, twisted around so gracefully that our own manoeuvres felt slow and clumsy.

We watched them shoot toward their breathing holes. I motioned to Rick to swim slowly up to a group of crabbies above. They parted almost as if to make way for him. All I could see then was his two dangling rubber fins gently waving among dozens of seal flippers.

Almost all the crabeaters bore scars on their flanks – twin parallel marks from wounds long healed. One theory has it that these scars are caused by leopard seal attacks when they're pups. But surely, I thought, not every single seal would be attacked. To be so prevalent, some scars must be caused by fighting among themselves – maybe mating is a very competitive activity. But they didn't act aggressively to us. When they gaped at us, it seemed to be to show excitement rather than to threaten. Often they were so close that we could distinguish the rows of special tricuspid (three-pronged) teeth adapted for catching krill. When a seal sucks in a mouthful of shrimps, excess water is sieved out through the gaps in its teeth.

We had two more dives with the crabbies, and then overnight, the group vanished. Perhaps the animals moved off in search of food – certainly, we never saw any krill when we were in the water with them.

Though we'd only spent a couple of hours with the seals, their gentle curiosity made me feel as if we had been accepted into their ranks for a moment. It was an intimate glimpse into their world. And the thought came to me – never to see a seal under water is like being denied the sight of a bird in the air.

Normanna Strait, Signy Island, South Orkney Islands, Antarctica, August.

Seal tableau. Rick kneels in the kelp on the top of Powell Rock, looking
at a crabbie, which seems as fascinated in him as he is in it.
The crabbie above is just heading up to the ice crack for a quick breath
of air, while the one on the right is twisting off a piece of seaweed – rather
like a cat chewing off a piece of grass.

WHEN THINGS HOT UP

Fight for Life

When I filmed at Churchill with Ewan McGregor, he thought the bears were "like men inside teddy bear suits", and this opening shot [previous page] always reminds me of his words.

The polar bears in the town are the most southerly population in the world. They're also the most well known; scientists have been studying them there for more than 35 years. They gather near Churchill in late October because the geography of Hudson Bay means that the pack ice of the refreezing sea bumps against the coast just near the town. So bears can then gain access to the ice and start hunting again after the thin pickings of summer.

While they're waiting for the ice to form, male bears engage in play-wrestling, testing their strength against each other in preparation for the following spring, when they'll be fighting in earnest for mating priorities with receptive females. Bouts of action can last for several minutes as the bears face up to each other on their hind legs, trying to push each other off balance. Then as quickly as this flares up, one bear will lie down, and peace is restored.

Studies at Churchill have highlighted all too clearly the effects of Arctic warming. Plants on the tundra are flowering earlier. The winter ice is thinner and more broken. The bears have a tough time hunting. Their response to the warming climate will be to go further north simply to survive.

So take yourselves and your children and go and see them while you can, because in all likelihood they won't be there in ten to fifteen years' time.

Churchill, Manitoba, Canada, late October, filming for *In the Wild – Polar Bears*, BBC/WNET.

Long Summers Kill Cubs

In 1996, Ian Stirling, the world's most experienced polar bear biologist, wrote the best-ever book on the whole ecology of polar bears. He called it simply *Polar Bears*. In 2011, he brought it bang up to date, incorporating the latest research. But he retitled it *Polar Bears – The Natural History of a Threatened Species*. A soberingly frightening sign of the new times.

This young polar bear cub had only been out of the den a matter of weeks, possibly only days. It just didn't have the strength to follow its mother as she looked for seals to hunt. The odds against it surviving may have been been laid down nine months before.

One of the outcomes of the warming of the Arctic over recent years has been longer ice-free summers. The sea ice is breaking up significantly earlier than it was 15 years ago, and it's not reforming until much later in the autumn.

Pregnant polar bears nowadays are going into their dens in poorer health than previously. They find it hard to hunt without a sea-ice platform, and the tough times of summer are lasting longer. In autumn, the screw is turned again because they have a much shorter time on the new sea ice to hunt for seals before they have to find somewhere to den up and give birth.

Many females enter their dens already hungry. They are giving birth to fewer cubs, and those cubs in turn are not as strong. The cubs' early days on the sea ice, when they have to keep up with their mother as she hunts for seals, has always been a crucial period of stress. These days the odds are even more stacked against them.

Hopen Island, Svalbard, March, filming for *Wildlife Special – Polar Bear*, BBC.

Strawberry Ice

Like a strawberry-flavoured slush drink, the slopes of the McLeod Glacier on Signy briefly turn bright red in summer. As the snow cover melts on the island, nutrients are carried from the thin soils by the water flowing over the glaciers. Simple algae in the snow are fertilised, and the plants multiply so much in the long days of sunlight that they become visible as a coloured layer on the ice. This species of alga is red, but others are green or pale brown, and where the melt streams run together into pools, the algae are concentrated and appear a deeper shade than normal.

Someone swore blind that as he walked across a reddened snowfield, he could smell watermelons with every squelching step he took. Frankly, I think that man must have been just too long down south.

McLeod Glacier, Signy Island, South Orkney Islands, Antarctica, March.

Gentoos Up, Adélies Down

Two indicators in this picture show how the Antarctic Peninsula's climate has warmed in recent years. The first is that gentoos occupy most of the nest sites. When I visited this colony more than 30 years ago, there were only a few gentoos incubating their eggs among a much larger number of Adélies. Now the Adélies have almost vanished.

What's happened here is typical of many rookeries down the length of the peninsula. The more northerly living, almost sub-Antarctic gentoos have been able to extend their range south as the winters have become milder and the sea-ice cover has diminished. Off the mid-region of the peninsula, the average winter temperature is six degrees warmer than it was 50 years ago – yes, a whole six degrees. Adélie numbers have crashed, the accepted reason being that their food supply has changed. The krill on which they depend have either moved away or have also dropped in abundance.

The second sign is that all the snow around the colony is tinted green, This is caused by the growth of snow algae. These micro-plants have been extra-fertilised by run-off from the penguin colony above, but growth has also been super-stimulated by the longer periods of rainy summer weather that is now the norm.

Port Charcot, Booth Island, Antarctic Peninsula, February, filming for *Life*, BBC.

Death by Muck

Sorry little chick – but your chances of making it are slim.

This Adélie is about a month old, and covered in downy feathers. But its down is just too matted with mud and guano from the rookery to be waterproof. With its insulation sorely compromised, the chick will be chilling too fast between feeds. It's highly doubtful that it'll make it to fledging.

I've seen some years on the Antarctic Peninsula when hardly any chicks survived. If too much pack ice persists around the colony in summer, that can have a severe impact on the efficiency of the feeding trips that the adults have to make for the chicks. Most penguins won't swim under heavy ice cover, and so they simply may not be able to reach the areas of krill.

It might be 30-50 kilometres to where they feed, and they usually cover such distances by 'porpoising' – swimming quickly with a short burst under water then a quick grabbed breath, the way a dolphin does. But that's not possible if the sea surface is covered by pack ice. Or they might feed, but then the ice forces so many detours on them that they use all their energy and food for themselves and so have nothing to offer the chick back at the rookery. Climate change doesn't always mean warming, it can result in more variability. So the challenge of years with heavy pack ice is still one the Adélies face.

Dream Island, Antarctic Peninsula, March, filming for *Life in the Freezer*, BBC.

All Change

It's interesting (but ultimately frightening) to look at climate change from the point of view simply of engineering principles, to see how it's affecting the polar zones.

Life-driven ecology has evolved what a designer would call negative feedback systems – systems that have inbuilt tendencies to keep the overall environment stable. A small change from what's normal in one place may bring changes in another. But those secondary changes tend to return the system to what it was before. So there's a little variation, but it never runs away in one direction for too long.

The problem that arises with warming in the polar regions is that small physical changes can lead to the very opposite – big *positive* feedbacks. Things may change initially by only a small amount, but that feeds back to make the change even greater, which then increases the rate of change even more.

Unbroken, snow-covered ice on the sea or land presents a pure white surface to the rays of the sun; 90 per cent of the heat and light is reflected. But if the temperature warms just a little, melting that snow and thinning that ice so that it's grey rather than white, then the darker colour will absorb more heat. More heat means more melting, and then the ▶

White's just right. Bears hunt best
with large expanses of sea ice.

Above
Last of the sea ice. Longer
summers mean earlier melts.

Left
Two extremes. The flat, white
floes reflect heat; the black,
open water soaks it in.

▶ grey ice thins to expose black water or rock. That's even darker, even better at absorbing heat, and so the melt factor increases once again. Bring in milder temperatures a little earlier every year, then the ice melts sooner, the summers become longer, the waters are warmer. So autumn sea-ice formation is delayed. The next year's winter ice is slower to form, so thinner, so melts sooner the next spring ... and so on.

It's scarily progressive when the change is being driven by increasing levels of CO_2 but there's a much bigger player coming into the picture in the Arctic. Millions of cubic kilometres of dead plant material frozen in the permafrost of Siberia, Alaska and Canada are now melting. Bacteria are rotting it, releasing methane. This gas is 15 times more effective as a greenhouse gas than CO_2 and so has the frightening potential to escalate the rate the planet is heating up.

The sea ice in the Arctic is thinning dramatically. The average thickness is only 60 per cent of what it was 30 years ago. Predictions of a summer when virtually all of the Arctic sea ice will melt are being made for earlier and earlier dates this century; 2020 now seems a safe but catastrophic bet. It will mean disaster for seals and polar bears that depend on the ice for breeding and feeding. ∎

FREEZE FRAME

SHOTS TO REMEMBER

The Perfect Polar Bear

Of all the pictures in this book, the one on the previous page is unique. If you love it, and if you want to continue thinking what an amazing encounter I must have had with a bear so close, then please don't read further.

Alone in this book, this fantastic picture is mostly just that – down to fantasy and imagination. The bear was real at one point, but that was long before I found him in a storeroom in a hotel in Resolute. When I took the photograph, he was stuffed.

A few weeks before, we'd had a request for a picture that showed a bear's keen sense of smell. I sent in one I had of a bear on his hind legs, because that's what bears sometimes do when they're hunting seals. They stand up to stick their noses higher, to better catch the faint scent of prey that might yet still be a mile away over the ice. But the image didn't convey enough of smell; it was returned marked "rejected".

Then, when coming back from an Arctic shoot, the weather delayed me for a few days in the small Inuit community of Resolute. Looking around my hotel for a better room to pick up the internet signal, I found this guy. He was a good specimen, professionally mounted, in a very lifelike pose – sort of half-rising to his feet as if about to pounce down on a seal lair. It was an unusual chance to have a look at a bear from super-close.

Click, click went the connections in my head. This animal in the black of winter lives by his sense of smell. Here was a photo opportunity to put a new perspective on the importance of that super-sensitive nose of his. So I pulled him over to the window, distorted the features of his handsome face by using a wide-angle lens from in close, Photoshopped the picture to remove all the distracting background and then added a final twinkle to his left eye.

I'd never sell it pretending it was a live bear, but promise me you won't tell anyone.

Resolute, Canadian Arctic, June.

Iceberg Flash

At the poles, when you're thinking photography, light is everything, and this picture says it all. I love it for its simplicity, its serenity and also its almost intangible feeling of transience. I knew that light was going to be on that berg for only seconds. I also realised the scene was so softly illuminated that in one exposure I could capture not only the orange on the ice but also details in the subtle blues of the icefall behind. Moments like that don't come along very often.

Neumayer Channel, Antarctic Peninsula, January, filming for *Life*, BBC.

Below the Blizzard

This four-week-old Weddell seal pup is sheltering in the lee of its mother, protected from the blizzard. The picture vividly says 'survival in extremes' because of the snow encrusting their faces and lying on their fur, and also the way the background is seen through the curtain of blowing snow. The key to the shot was for me to lie low, down at the seals' level. Not just because that's always where you have the best angle for any subject – intimate and at the same eye height – but in this case, the 'blizzard' was, in fact, only blowing up to half a metre above the snow surface.

It wasn't a full-on hoolie, but it was the photographer's perfect storm – the one that says it all without being it all. The wind was strong enough at the boundary layer to pick up the ice particles so they rushed blurred past the lens, while the dark seal bodies meant this moving snow was visible in the lens. If I'd stayed at normal standing height, I'd never have seen any of this. It would have been merely two slightly snow-powdered seals lying on the ice.

McMurdo Sound, Antarctica, November, filming for *Life*, BBC.

Sealing mode. The pod shifted up a gear when they went hunting in the loose pack ice. They spread out, and individuals began looking for seals. Their actions were tighter, more disciplined, full of menacing purpose.

The Seal Killers

Thirty-two years and ten days after I first heard about it, I finally witnessed my Antarctic holy grail: killer whales taking seals off ice floes, using coordinated attacks that showed what I can only call super-intelligence.

Vague rumours of the behaviour first surfaced in January 1977. People at the Argentinian base in the Melchior Islands talked of orcas hunting seals on ice floes in the channels around the station.

We looked for the behaviour when filming *Life in the Freezer* and might have came close to a kill when we found big strips of whale blubber floating at a berg, with orcas patrolling nearby. But fog patches hid any action.

We searched again while filming for *The Blue Planet* and *Life*, and took a big step forward on *Life* when we proved we could follow an orca pod with a ship for almost 24 hours without disturbing them. But at 1am, it was too gloomy to see them properly, and we lost them.

A year later, for *Frozen Planet*, we would go south a little earlier in the summer, when there was still 24 hours of good daylight. That season we were rewarded with the most spectacular behaviour I've ever seen.

Antarctic Peninsula, January, filming for *Frozen Planet*, BBC.

119

Above and opposite
Just looking. Killer whales are very selective about their prey.
The way they 'spyhop' near the floes suggests they are
checking out the seals as you or I would – by simply looking.
In both these cases, the seals are crabeaters, which are
fast, flexible and capable of inflicting serious injury.
The killer whales leave them alone. Their targets are the less
aggressive, blubber-rich Weddells.

Above
Fate sealed. There's a chilling inevitability about
the outcome once a Weddell seal's identity has been
confirmed. The orcas swim round the floe several
times, seeming to assess it and decide on a strategy.

Previous page
Targeting. The killers spyhop to make doubly sure
that the sleeping seal is a Weddell.

Synchronising. The killers swim off to prepare to
carry out the final, dramatic act.

Left
Charge. The killers swim abreast towards the floe from about 40 metres away, tails beating together. After judging the size of the floe, they somehow decide whether to dive together and make a wave that breaks up the ice from underneath or whether to create a different kind of wave, one that peaks just before the floe so that it washes over the ice, carrying the seal into the water.

Above
Finality. Seals may manage to stay on the floe for one or two waves, but eventually they're washed into the water. We didn't see any escape alive.

No Booby Prize for Snow Petrel

We used to have a competition on base for the worst wildlife photograph anyone had taken during the year. The Daphne Machin Goodall Prize was in honour of the author of the same name.

This well-intentioned lady had been south on one of the early tour ships and had produced a book full of frankly awful photographs – compositionally challenged, exposed so that all the scenes were muddily dark or blindingly white. Her captions were also strewn with errors. Page 17, for example, featured "Giant skua chicks". As far as we knew, no such species ever nested in the Antarctic. Skuas yes, giant petrels yes, giant skuas, sorry no.

You couldn't, of course, set out with the deliberate intention of taking an awful shot. It was only a valid entry if the person with the camera was truly trying for a good photograph.

Andy Turner entered one year. He put up a shot of what looked like a boringly lumpy sea, under slate grey skies, with the horizon slanted just enough to be noticeable. At first we could see no wildlife at all. Then Andy pointed out a small black shape in the upper left-hand corner. Zooming into the picture, we could just make out the fin of a killer whale. He clinched the prize with his next comment: "I'm calling this one 'Closing In for the Kill'." It was a very worthy winner indeed (unlike my snow petrel opposite, which wouldn't have come anywhere near the top).

Antarctic Peninsula, January, filming for *Life*, BBC.

Up She Came

"What I want is empty, flat, virgin ice. Then in a big close-up, this massive black conning tower will rise phallic-like from below, cracking the ice and emerging ever higher, backlit against the low sun."

We'd just travelled in the Royal Navy submarine HMS *Tireless* under the North Pole sea ice from Greenland to Alaska, and now I wanted to film her counterpart from the US Navy coming up through the ice. I was describing my dream shot to the US naval officer in charge of topside operations, fully expecting to be told that, despite their obviously sophisticated equipment strewn all around us on the ice, my suggestions were just impractical.

"And what direction would you like the boat to be facing?" he asked. I was about to see my hi-tech problem had a very low-tech solution.

He turned to a rating: "OK, you know the drill. You've done this before for the TV guys."

He drilled a small hole through the thin ice and dropped a hydrophone pinger down into the water. "That'll bring the boat in close," I was assured.

One of the ratings asked, "You sure about where you want that sail up, and where the bows should point?" Yes I was. The rating began shovelling aside the light covering of snow on top of the ice, and in a minute or so he'd marked out a big arrowhead and shaft.

It was gloriously simple. The sub zeroed in on the pinger, and using its underwater cameras, the skipper could easily see the outline of the arrow through the thin ice. He stopped the boat directly under the end of the shaft, pointed the bows to the arrowhead, and up she came.

Easy when you know how.

Beaufort Sea, Alaska, March.

The Science of Bubbles

Being the biggest of the penguins perhaps means that emperors are just naturally the most confident – they were certainly the easiest to approach in the water. They swam close by me with majestic indifference. Using their flippers for propulsion and their stiff tail feathers as rudders, they're beautifully adapted for diving effortlessly into the depths. Their dives usually last about 5 minutes, sometimes down to 300 metres, where they feed on krill, squid or perhaps fish.

Researchers measured the hydrodynamic drag of a penguin in a kind of water-filled wind tunnel by having it swim against a steadily increasing current. They worked with gentoos, a species somewhere in size between an emperor and an Adélie. They found that its body was so streamlined that it only produced the same underwater drag as would a 10p piece. No wonder penguins can change direction as if on rails.

While their descent has a lazy grace, their arrival back at the surface is jet-propelled. They come up from the black water, leaving trails of bubbles behind them, flying (you couldn't call it swimming) so fast that they come clean out of the water. No problem for them to clear an ice edge a couple of metres high.

The sequence we filmed for *The Blue Planet* raised oohs and aahs from the audience, but it was even more satisfying when it raised scientific eyebrows ten years later. Images of these emperor penguins streaking to the surface, bubbles streaming behind them, led to a whole new thinking about how and why these bubbles appeared.

The old idea was that the bubbles simply came out from under the feathers, because as the penguins accelerated up through the shallows, the pressure of the water next to their bodies was reduced. So in the same way that bubbles form in the water around a boat propeller when it's turning rapidly, so bubbles would appear next to the penguin. It was just something that happened as they swam fast. It was physics, not biology.

But it turned out not to be as simple as that.

Scientists took a closer look at hundreds of single frames from our film and saw that, as the penguins came up, fine bubbles were emerging continuously from their plumage, forming a smooth layer over their bodies and making the bubble trails. But when the scientists did the maths (lots of maths), they worked out that these bubbles were actually helping the penguins to zoom *faster* through the water than they could without them. The bubbles were acting as lubrication.

And even more remarkable, it's the emperor itself who is controlling when to release the bubbles. The air is trapped in the thick layer of downy feathers close to the penguin's body, beneath the tougher outer feathers. As it ascends, the emperor is able to relax the muscles at the base of its feathers and so release the air. It's then able to gain the fraction more speed that gives it that little more jump height, which might just grant it the tiny advantage that could mean it escapes the leopard seal which might be chasing it up onto the ice.

And we might not know any of that if I hadn't had some great times floating off the Ross Ice Shelf for *The Blue Planet*.

Cape Washington, Ross Sea, November, filming for *The Blue Planet*, BBC.

Meet the Minke

We had perfect conditions to look for killer whales. In flat calm like this, not only can you see them miles away, you can also clearly hear them blowing at the surface. But on this occasion it was a minke causing the blows and ripples. These whales are usually tricky to film. They surface erratically, change direction while they're under water, never hang around very long. But this individual seemed fascinated by the boat, perhaps by the steady, unchanging tick-over note of the inboard diesel engine, or just because we were lying motionless in the water.

It circled us several times no more than 20 metres out, and from the elevation of the wheelhouse roof, I had a great view of its white chin rising from the black water. The whale came up at a very shallow angle, and so I had time to press the shutter when it was just centimetres sub-surface – a once-in-a-lifetime moment when a whole lot of things came together to offer a very special image.

Marguerite Bay, Antarctic Peninsula, February, filming for *Life*, BBC.

Cameraman's Holiday

Illampu was the highest peak in the Cordillera Real, according to
the guidebook. But the book failed to say exactly how high. The best
we could track down was somewhere between 6000 and 6500
metres. High enough.

After finishing a contract in Antarctica in 1984, Paul, Dave and I went
climbing in the range of Andean peaks that runs northwest from
La Paz in Bolivia. Information about the route itself was almost
non-existent, and looking up at the mountain from below, it was
obvious that with so many ice falls and seracs to be navigated on the
main face, the way up was going to change from year to year.

But we had perfect climbing weather, slept in a crevasse on the way
up, topped out the following day. I grabbed this shot as we crossed
the main bergschrund – the big open crevasse high on the slopes,
where moving glacier ice separates from the static ice higher up that's
stuck to the rock. A wonderful airy place, above the clouds. The shot
brings back all the feeling of excitement that I had – treading new
paths, heightened awareness, good company. It's one of my favourite
climbing pictures, and thank goodness for Dave's red mitts.

Cordillera Real, Bolivia, May.

FREEZE FRAME

CLOSE CALLS

So Long, Skidoo

George and I took a skidoo out one Sunday morning to go and look for Weddell seals off North Point. We were travelling light and fast, both of us on the same machine. I suppose we really should have noticed the suspiciously greyish patch of ice just off the penguin rookery, but the first realisation of trouble was when we felt our speed decreasing and I sensed the rear end of the snow machine dropping downwards.

I glanced around. We had almost a rooster tail of slush being kicked up behind us as the drive tracks chewed the thin ice. George immediately steered us for a patch of thicker ice, but we both knew with a horrible inevitability that we weren't going to make it. We were slowing down too much. In the end it was like the graceful abandoning of the snow-machine *Titanic*. We came to a complete stop. The back end was under water in seconds, but there was still time for both of us to step off and onto the ice, which was just thick enough to take our weight but not the machine's. It gurgled into the depths while we watched.

It was just a 20-minute walk back to base. Kevin the mechanic watched us arrive on foot. Only half an hour before, he'd seen us zooming away on one of his machines.

"Problems out there?" he asked. George came back quick as a flash: "Nothing serious, just flooded the engine."

Two days later the ice had thickened enough for us to go safely back to the spot. We cut a hole, dived, put lifting bags on the machine and brought her to the surface. A full strip-down of the engine, and she was as good as new.

Signy Island, South Orkney Islands, Antarctica, August.

Shooting Guillemots, Hitting a Walrus

I vividly remember taking this shot – not for the image itself, rather for the immediate aftermath.

I'd been in the water for about an hour, slowly swimming closer to the birds, trying to catch the moment of their synchronous dive. I'd taken maybe ten shots and had the Nikonos to my eye for an eleventh. I was vertical, treading water, when suddenly – with absolutely no warning – I was grabbed very tightly around my upper thighs. I looked down, and under my right arm was the head of a walrus. Purely instinctively, I thumped both fists hard down and kicked like hell.

The walrus let go. I guess he was as surprised as I'd been (though probably not as scared). He swam off a little way and then turned to look at me with his curious piggy eyes. He was a juvenile, with tusks maybe half a metre long.

I covered the short distance back to the ice edge in less time than it's taken to read this far. It was only when I hauled myself onto the ice that the adrenaline really kicked in. The walrus had grabbed me in exactly the same way it would take an unwary seal – from underneath. It would then kill the seal by drowning it, crushing it between its tusks or sucking its brains out. Walruses have very strong cheek muscles that can exert a powerful suction, normally used when they're getting clams out of a gravelly seabed but equally useful for quickly killing a seal.

It's the only incident in my life that brings me out in a cold sweat every time I recall it. The element of total surprise, the speed of it all, how different the outcome would have been had he held on when I hit his head rather than letting go. I would have drowned within seconds if he'd taken me under.

Lancaster Sound Floe Edge, Canadian Arctic, June, filming for *Arctic Kingdom – Life at the Edge*, National Geographic.

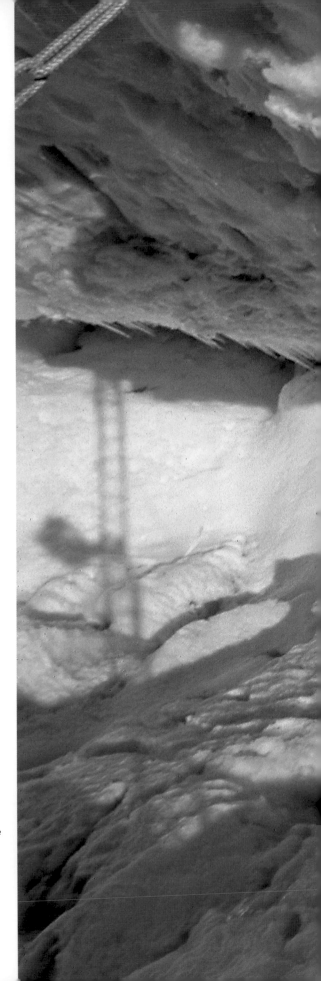

Experiencing Everest

The view is literally staggering. It really is like being in an aircraft. I can probably see a couple of hundred kilometres. But I'm exhausted. I can put down the tripod when I reach my orange tent, only 100 metres higher. It's no more than ten minutes' easy climb away – if I were at sea level. But I'm almost 7000 metres up on the North Col of Everest, and reaching that tent is going to take me well over an hour of lung-burstingly painful effort.

Altitude is a great leveller. Most fit people could reach 4000 metres without a problem. Sure, there would be fatigue and a certain light-headedness, but if you take it easy, you'll make it. But pushing on half as high again up to 6000 metres begins to take its toll. You'd certainly have to spend time on the way up simply acclimatising, resting for several days, 'walking high and sleeping low' on others. So some days your walk might take you to a new high point, but then you'd drop down lower for the night.

Above 6000 metres, we're talking altitude effects that seriously threaten mind and body. This is where, if you ignore the rules and push too hard, you may well become one more high-mountain statistic.

On the Nepalese side of Everest, base camp (BC) is a popular trekking destination, and in peak months, such as May, trekkers and climbers may number 500 or more. That's as far as your modest trekker's permit will allow you to go, but since the next stage of the mountain proper entails the Khumbu Icefall, most folk wouldn't go any further anyway. ▶

Crazy crossing. If you think it's scary stepping over a crevasse like this, imagine what it would be like trying to make it over *without* the ladder. I was climbing the Khumbu Icefall at almost 6000 metres on the Nepalese side of Everest. There was a hand line to grab hold of as I inched across, but all the same, the normal advice is *not* to look down...

▶ The icefall rises for 800 metres above BC, a 'chossy', steep mess of tottering serac ice towers and deep crevasses that have claimed the lives of more climbers than any other part of the mountain. I picked a route through it three times on one filming trip, and each time it felt like Russian roulette.

On the northern, Tibetan side, the approach is along the spectacular Rongbuk Valley. The enormous bulk of Everest squats square in front of you like a Buddha, with all the expedition tents at BC pitched like supplicants on the flat area at the end of the receding glacier.

Advance Base Camp (ABC) is a further 12-hours walk up the valley to 6400 metres. What surprised me was that I reached there without having set foot on any snow whatsoever. The trek had all been on dirt tracks that wound up through the lateral moraines and across the slopes.

It's a very strange feeling that permeates BC and ABC sites during the climbing season. There are throngs of people at times, the odd noisy party, the crackle of radio coms from tents talking to their climbers higher up, lots of satphones with climbers saying good night to their children and girlfriends. People drop by to chat. Some are friendly; others are just trying to pick your brains. It has the feel of a big village.

But there is always tension just under the surface, an awareness that the next news you may hear of the person you met and chatted with yesterday is that they're missing or dead higher up – a rockfall, an avalanche, a case of cerebral oedema, a simple slip – suddenly   ▶

Bridging that gap. In the climbing season, Sherpas first set up and then maintain the ladders that bridge the major crevasses on the icefalls on both the north and south sides of Everest. Without them it would take far longer to climb the hill. Crossings can be quite hairy as icefalls aren't stable. A ladder can be gently inclined and horizontal one morning but barely attached at one end and tilting crazily by the afternoon.

▶ you realise where you are and what you're trying to do.

On the highest Everest climbing camps, poised for the final push to the top, you really might as well be on another planet. The margins between survival and death are so very, very slender, so much can just come down to purely fickle fate, and it's not always the apparently best equipped who manage the full trip.

Everest comes with a weight of history that presses down on everyone who ventures onto its slopes. That can combine with your own feelings, so you psych yourself out of the game before you really start. No matter who you are, Everest will change you.

While I never saw a dead body myself, the higher you go on the mountain, the more you come across them. 'Come across' may sound just too matter of fact, but I can think of no more apt a phrase.

When filming Russell Brice for Discovery's *Everest Extreme* series, I heard him on the radio at Camp 1 speaking to his climbers higher up. "It's important to make Green Boots with more than half your oxygen supplies," was the gist of what he said at one point. Up there on the route to the summit was a body with green climbing boots, lying on a windy spot on the ridge where little snow accumulated. How many seasons ago he had died, no one could exactly remember. Now he was being referred to with apparently no more thought than a signpost would be given on your way to your destination. Strangely, it didn't feel callous, just practical. Up that high, where most climbers' brains ▶

Hell to Heaven. First impressions of Tibetan-side Everest Base Camp — cold, dry, dusty, windy, breathless, miserable. Six weeks later and you're back after a long spell much higher on the hill. Now BC is a gentle place that's warm, oxygen-rich and redolent of luxury. As the song (almost) goes, "What a difference a month makes."

▶ are barely functioning, their own survival depends on their concentrating totally on themselves. Deep thoughts about what might have been the fate of others can wait until you're safely off the hill.

Everyone has a limit beyond which they cannot go. It's determined partly by your fitness but also by your genetics. It's as if we all have a max limit programmed into our bodies. And just like your investments, proof of past performance at sea level is no guarantee of future performance up high. The unlikeliest, fittest people can grind to a halt well below the summit, while that little guy whose accent few can understand may just manage to keep things in focus.

The highest I ever went was 8014 metres to the summit of Shishapangma, but my two trips to Everest stand out because, of course, that hill is *the* most charismatic peak in the world.

I'm not sure I'd actually have the stamina to top out on Everest, because long periods around 6000 metres or higher cause me first to lose my appetite and second to sleep much less than normally. It's truly a shit way to live, and on those odd days when you feel as if you're coping, it's almost a sign that it's time you pushed yourself harder.

I can keep going for six to seven weeks, but then the crash comes. Since summiting on Everest is closer to a ten-week climb, my get-up-and-go just gets up and leaves that bit too soon.

But despite all that, as the horizontal wild polar places challenge ▶

Blizzard base. You feel the altitude here at
Advance Base Camp on the Tibetan side of
Everest, with the infamous NE ridge behind.
The summit is just out of view behind the
highest point of the ridge. This is not a day
for climbing. That wind would make for
a lethal chill on the upper slopes.

▶ and inspire me like no others, I also enjoy the cold vertical zones. Easing step by tentative step across a crevasse ladder while climbing through the Khumbu Icefall on the Nepalese side, watching the last of the orange alpen glow fade from the north face at sunset, pausing for breath on some steep slope, doubled over my ice axe and coughing up what feels like pieces of my lungs, while Sherpas seemingly run up the slope past me – it's very satisfying to have seen and done all that. And when the filming and climbing are finished, there's such a depth of sheer relief knowing I'm safe and will soon be on the way home.

On each of the three high trips I made, I burst into tears at the end. It was wonderfully cathartic, walking away and just letting the tears run, completely unashamed that anyone might be watching.

There's a classic book written by Apsley Cherry-Garrard entitled *The Worst Journey in the World*. It's about the trip that he and two others from Scott's party made in 1911 from their base at Cape Evans to the emperor penguin colony at Cape Crozier, 70 miles away. They did it in the total blackness of winter, manhauling their sledge, in temperatures down to -60°C and winds up to 70 mph. It's a *very* apt title.

In the book, C-G offers the pithy observation that "Polar exploration is at once the cleanest and most isolated way of having a bad time which has been devised" – words that very well apply to being on Everest.

Nepal and Tibet, May and June, filming both times for Discovery Channel.

Line-up. This is a procession of climbers making their way from the camp on the Everest North Col up to Camp 2, which is just above where the rock starts at the top of the snow slope. It looks no distance at all, and it's only 500 metres higher, which you'd think is nothing for a day's climbing. But you're doing well if you make it in less than five hours.

Insanity Island

I could barely hear Dave's shouts above the machine-gun rattle of the gravel sandblasting my tent. If I hadn't been actually sitting inside, with a few big camera cases for extra ballast, the whole thing would have gone up in the air long ago. Finally there was a lull in the storm just long enough to make out Dave yelling, "Welcome to Zavodovski, mate!"

The eight islands that make up the South Sandwich group are way out in the southern Atlantic, about 2500 kilometres southeast of the tip of South America. They're in the latitude that sailors refer to as the 'filthy fifties', where gales sweep uninterrupted around the southern oceans. We'd arrived three days before to huge swells breaking onshore, and the cliffs that virtually ringed Zavodovski had us wondering if we'd make it onto land at all. A couple of weeks before, in the Falklands, someone had said: "You'll never do it without a helicopter." I'd laughed at the time, but now I wasn't so sure.

We were there for *The Blue Planet* to film a sequence about the biggest chinstrap and macaroni penguin colony in the world, and the only one on the slopes of an active volcano. But we wouldn't achieve anything if we couldn't make it ashore.

We bobbed and rolled around the island in the *Golden Fleece*, looking for landing sites. Waves three metres high pounded the only stretch of beach. The rest of the shoreline was steep cliffs, split here and there by narrow gullies. In one of those, a climbable vertical crack offered a place where it was feasible to jump ashore. ▶

Volcano ahoy. The old explorers in their ships said that, in thick fog, you could tell you were approaching some islands by the smell of guano coming downwind from the penguin rookeries. With Zavodovski, it was the smoke and fumes from the active volcano that gave it away.

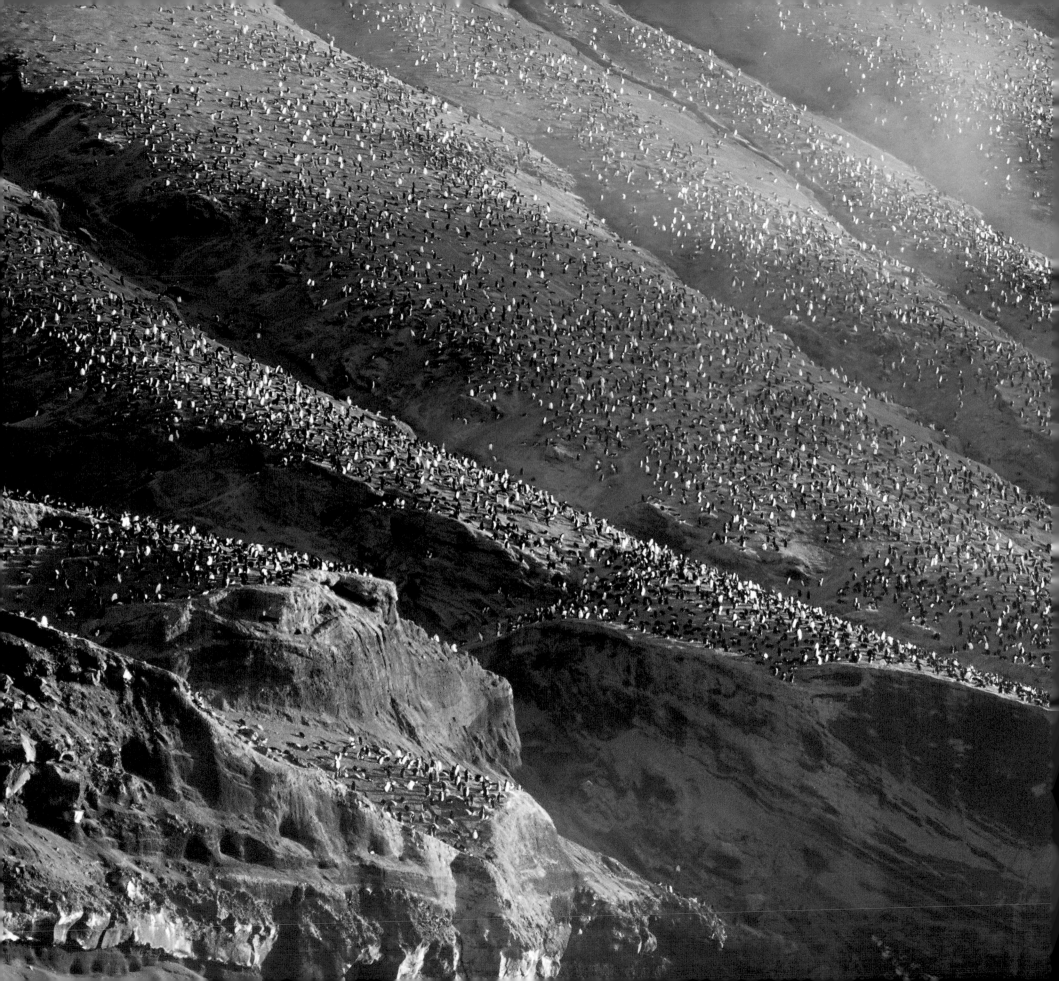

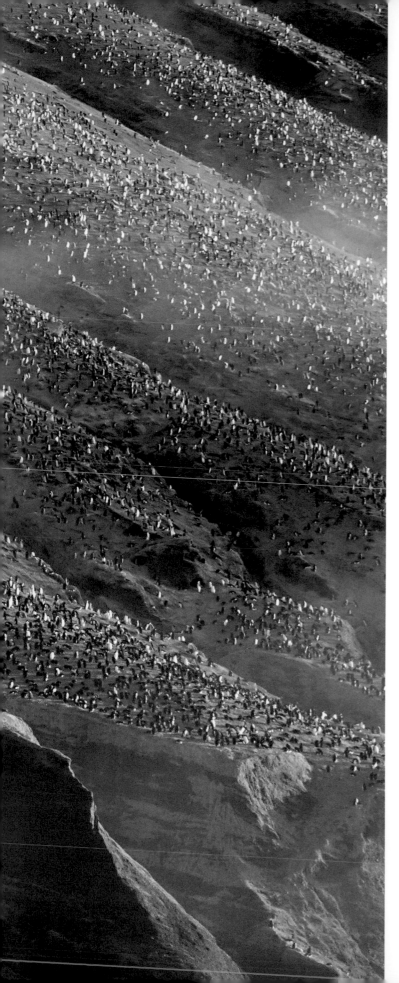

Smoking. On a rare calm afternoon, a blue smoky haze ghosts over the thousands of penguins nesting on the slopes of Zavodovski. I don't know when the volcano last erupted in earnest, but the air always smells of sulphur.

▶ Put the nose of the inflatable against the rock, wait until the top of the swell, scramble off into the crack and haul yourself up the 10 metres to the top.

A little way along, an overhanging rock jutted out over the sea. We could drop a rope down from there. People in the inflatable below tied on equipment, and the man on the rock pulled it up. When the swell was big, it was quite a hairy operation, and at times it did have the feel of a one-way trip.

We had to make sure we were self-contained, with several days' worth of supplies on shore, because getting off was clearly going to be impossible in bad conditions. I was remembering that as I gripped the tent poles tighter, so they wouldn't snap in the wind.

Zavodovski was never easy, but the spectacular nature of the location more than compensated for all the difficulties. Hundreds of thousands of penguins came ashore every day to feed their chicks, no matter what the weather. In one of the gullies, rafts of chinstrap penguins would surface in the massive swell and then dive down as a big wave rolled in, before shooting out of the water as the wave peaked. When they mistimed their jump, they'd be battered off the rocks. Somehow they survived, ready to try once more.

In some ways, the steep cliffy parts were less treacherous landing sites than the beach area. We walked that way the day after a massive storm and found hundreds of penguins trapped under big rocks. ▶

▶ The force of the swell had squeezed them into nooks and crannies, from where they just couldn't extricate themselves, and the boulders were way too heavy for us to move. We just had to leave them.

There was one location in particular on Zavodovski where we wanted to film, up on a shoulder, where penguins were nesting against a backdrop of smoking volcanic fumaroles. But this meant landing on a narrow beach, which so far had proved impossible because of the swells. Every day we offered up prayers to the wind gods, and finally the miracle happened: not just calm but blue skies as well.

We almost threw the gear off the outcrop of rock into the inflatable in our haste to motor round the corner to check out the other beach. Conditions were almost perfect when we were finally dropped off. Four of us began to walk the gear along the beach to where the slope would allow us up to the nesting shoulder.

As we headed along the narrow, stony shoreline, we could hear the singing, then splintering noise of small (and not so small) stones falling down from the unstable ash slopes above and smashing to pieces on the rocks of the beach. I began to feel I was in the opening scene of *Indiana Jones and the Temple of Doom*. If the wind didn't get us, some other hazard would. If the small stones missed, a big round one would flatten me.

After all this, it turned out an easy scramble up to the shoulder – truly an awesome location: penguins and chicks in an unreal landscape of ▶

Nursery heights. You can make out the *Golden Fleece*
anchored just offshore in centre-right of the picture,
and also the beach that we traversed before climbing up
the slopes to the chinstraps.

Ice gathering. Chinstraps are dotted about on this berg a mile or so offshore of Zavodovski.

▶ smouldering vents, the ground streaked with yellow sulphur stains. In places on the slopes, the hot gases had eroded red ash-covered lumps of ice into fantastic shapes.

I wondered if the chinstraps here had a shorter incubation period than elsewhere. Did their eggs hatch a little quicker with the natural underfloor heating?

I could have stayed filming for several hours, but the radio crackled. News from the *Fleece*: the swell was building, and maybe we should think about heading back. A very sensible call.

We had a lot of fun manoeuvring ourselves and our gear off that beach. What had been a sheltered corner was now a swirling maelstrom. The waves had become much bigger. It was impossible to keep the bows of the inflatable facing into the swell even with one of us on each side and the others loading. It was only a matter of time before the inevitable happened.

I felt a big swell lift me clear of the bottom. Then in slow motion, all turned dark as I was sucked under the boat and it passed over my head.

I washed out the other side next to Dave, who told me to "stop pissing about and get back to your own place".

All of us were soaked to the skin, but that didn't matter at all because we were on our way back with great footage in the can.

Zavodovski, South Sandwich Islands, January, filming for The Blue Planet, BBC.

Jumping the Crack

The huskies in an Inuit dog team are the toughest dogs in the world. They're often not as big as you'd expect, but when harnessed together, they have a pulling power that's astounding. And all that power is never more needed than when coming back across the sea ice late in the spring as the ice is starting to crack up.

You may be following the same track as a couple of days earlier, but the melting ice is like a giant jigsaw where the pieces slowly change shape so they no longer fit tightly together. Cracks called leads develop, and the dog driver needs all his skill to steer the sledge towards places where the lead is narrow enough for the dogs and sledge to cross. An error of judgement or hesitation by the first dogs, and the sledge will lose speed and go into the water.

In this shot, the crack is just that bit too wide – some of the dogs have jumped over but some have gone in. The sledge is still moving, but the driver is trying to push it sideways so it goes over at the narrower part of the crack to the left of the dogs.

He succeeded, the dogs kept on running, and I had my work cut out to catch up with them after taking the picture.

Qaanaak, Greenland, June, filming for *Human Planet*, BBC.

David A. and Death by Skidoo

In 2001, I was asked by producer Mike Salisbury to do a shoot in Svalbard on Arctic foxes for the *The Life of Mammals* series. I was really pleased to be offered this chance – a wonderful location that I knew well, charismatic but accessible subjects, and working with one of the best producers in the BBC Natural History Unit. But best of all, it was my first chance to film David Attenborough presenting a piece to camera.

Though he and I had been involved with several series since *The Trials of Life* back in 1989, and I'd met David often on location and at wildlife festivals, I had never been entrusted with filming him. You can draw your own conclusions from that.

The shoot entailed us driving out on snow machines with sledges onto the sea ice every day for a week or so, tracking and finding the foxes and then filming their behaviour. David, of course and as always, was ready to do all he could to make the sequence work for the screen, and part of that was for him to do a piece to camera, talking about the foxes. Mike suggested that, as an introduction to David's search, we should have some shots of him driving the snow machine over rough ice.

David is rightly regarded as the best-known natural history broadcaster on the planet. His sureness of touch with the spoken word is legendary. But he'd be the first to admit his confidence doesn't extend to snow-machine driving.

Using the telephoto zoom lens, I cracked off the shots of him from a distance with no problem. But I knew we'd also want a dramatic, wide, low-angle shot of the machine passing by me and leaving the frame. And for that I needed to lie on the snow and have David come past me at speed, very close.

David doesn't usually need more than a couple of takes to get his delivery right, but it took quite a few attempts before he'd come close enough and fast enough for me. I remember him calling over at one point: "Imagine the fuss if I drove over you. All those BBC forms we'd have to fill in."

When I asked him much later if he would sign my copy of the series' book, he thought for a moment before jotting down on the title page what must have been his most vivid memories from that shoot we did together: "For Doug, who so fearlessly faced death by skidoo. With gratitude. David."

Svalbard, Ny Ålesund, April, filming for *The Life of Mammals*, BBC.

Time Slices

During my winter at Halley, we often drove the 20 kilometres down to the emperor penguins on the coast, following the route we'd marked with empty oil drums every 250 metres or so.

The snow surface of the ice shelf was essentially featureless except for a few areas near the coast, crisscrossed by meandering ribbons of slightly shadowed snow. These were crevasses – cracks in the ice sheet – and they could vary in width from barely hairline to several metres. They posed a significant danger in cloudy conditions, when the contrast was so poor you couldn't see them. But on fine, sunny days, we could confidently probe their edges. Where they were safe enough to explore, we dropped climbing ropes into their depths and abseiled down.

The parallel walls glowed deep blue from within and were finely striped, each layer marking the previous year's snowfall, long since compacted into ice. Fifteen metres down and we might be gazing at ice several hundred years old. It was colder than up on top, and the feeling was one of utter stillness and strange permanence.

It might have been claustrophobic if it hadn't been so breathtakingly beautiful. Our voices were muffled. Without meaning to, we found ourselves speaking in whispers.

British Antarctic Survey Research Station, Halley, Brunt Ice Shelf, Weddell Sea, Antarctica, October.

The Night I Felt Like a Seal

This book wouldn't be complete without the story about my closest encounter with a polar bear.

I was travelling with Andrew, my Inuit guide. It was early March, still very cold. I was on a long trip for National Geographic, looking for bears. We'd seen one on an earlier shoot, but I'd missed the moment when he'd grabbed a seal. So we were still hoping for that part of the sequence.

We'd camped for the night near Prince Leopold Island. I could hear the ice creaking and cracking as the tide rose and fell. Good place, I reckoned, for bears to come hunting. They would know the seals used those cracks as breathing holes. I was also thinking how fearsomely cold it was in the tent, even with the sleeping bag pulled over my head.

Eight hours later I woke to the sensation of something repeatedly touching my feet. For a few seconds I lay quiet. Andrew was snoring on his side of the tent. Who was it then outside? Slowly I emerged from the depths of my sleeping bag and looked down to the far end of the tent.

Silhouetted through the backlit canvas was the unmistakable profile of a very big bear. A tiny corner of my caribou-fur sleeping mat was twitching as he pawed at it. I wouldn't say I was scared, but I did feel rather concerned. It's one thing to be separated from a bear by the wood of cabin walls. But flimsy tent material?

I nudged Andrew awake, who was remarkably laid back. His suggestion was: "Stick your head out the tent flap. He'll go away."

To which I could only reply, "How about you stick your head outside the tent, Andrew."

As ever, he was right. This bear was so wary that, in the time it took us to pull our boots on and look outside, he was ambling across the ice away from the camp.

Lancaster Sound, Canadian Arctic, April, filming for *Arctic Kingdom – Life at the Edge*, National Geographic.

The Near-death Proposal

This was the view as we lifted off in the helicopter. We'd just recovered the last of our gear from our camp, pitched on what had been – 24 hours before – solid sea ice. I took the picture from the rescue helicopter on its way to drop the three of us and our equipment safely back on terra firma.

Sue Flood and I, with Olayuk our guide, were on assignment for *The Blue Planet*, looking for narwhals and belugas. We were camped on the frozen sea ice at the edge of Lancaster Sound in the Canadian Arctic, a safe kilometre or so back from the edge. For a week we'd been relishing round-the-clock sunshine, filming at the floe edge where the solid ice meets the open water. The previous day had been a long one, 19 hours non-stop, and we'd returned at 1am in thickening fog.

Four hours later, I was awakened by muted mutterings. Olayuk was outside our tent, talking softly to me. In between words of Inuktitut, I could hear him mention "open water". I thought at first he was trying to make plans for later in the day, but his tone had an air of urgency.

I stuck my head outside – and realised immediately why Olayuk was concerned. The solid ice around us had broken into floes, dark open water was lapping only metres from the tent, and many ominous cracks were snaking blackly into the white fogginess.

I realised right away that there was no way we were going to be able to drive our snow machines to safety. In fact, at that particular moment, there was no way we were going to be rescued at all. ▶

The remains. The scene first thing in the morning when we saw our snow-machine tracks leading into the water and realised the ice had disintegrated.

Help! On the radio, calling
for assistance.

Relief. Smiles all round when we
knew the helicopter was on its way.

Help. The cavalry
has arrived.

▶ We were on an ice floe about 30 metres in diameter, and only by sheer luck was all our gear still on it. We couldn't see further than 50 metres in any direction – it was a white-out with thick fog. Two thoughts rushed in. How the hell had we slept through all this happening? And how were we going to get off? I knew floes like ours could break into pieces no bigger than dinner plates in minutes, once a swell rose.

Luckily, we still had a means of communication: Olayuk's HF radio. Within an hour, we had made contact with Arctic Bay, the nearest village, about 110 kilometres away.

"Don't worry, we're praying for you," was the message back. Encouraging, I thought. But more practical would be for them to patch us through to Dave Malloly, the flight operations director at Resolute, a community 170 kilometres distant, where there was a helicopter.

By another piece of good fortune, I had been talking to Dave on the radio only a few days earlier, discussing the possibility of some helicopter time to do aerials. He had said he'd see if one was available for the Sunday afternoon.

My conversation now started, "You remember that helo that might be ready in the afternoon? Any chance of sending him out a little earlier, please? We have a bit of a situation here." The key is to sound cool in situations like that, even with the dinner plates threatening.

Dave of course immediately agreed, though we did have to wait a

further five hours for the freezing drizzle to pass through Resolute and the fog to lift over us.

While the sea stayed calm, we prepared for the worst. We had a small plastic rowing boat, big enough for the three of us and our most valuable possessions. Sue and I loaded cameras and some spare clothing. Olayuk on the other hand took the stove and about a square metre of fresh *muktuk*, the skin and blubber from a small whale he had hunted the previous week. You could tell a lot about our cultures from our priorities.

When people ask me now what my favourite sound is, I usually start by talking about a beluga whistling at me under water. But the clatter of those rotor blades approaching to rescue us comes a close second.

We had a great pilot. As it was a full rescue trip, he could have said it's one trip to shore and you leave the gear. But he agreed to do a number of ferry flights with all our stuff slung in a cargo net. That took another couple of hours.

And in the time that we were waiting for the help, I also made my marriage proposal to Sue. This was not, as some black-humoured friends have suggested, "because you expected to die", but because I had been waiting for a special moment. And they don't come much more special than that.

North Admiralty Inlet, Baffin Island, Canadian Arctic, June, filming for *The Blue Planet*.

The break-up. As we left on the helicopter, we could
see just how much the ice had broken-up.

FREEZE FRAME

CHARACTERS
I HAVE KNOWN

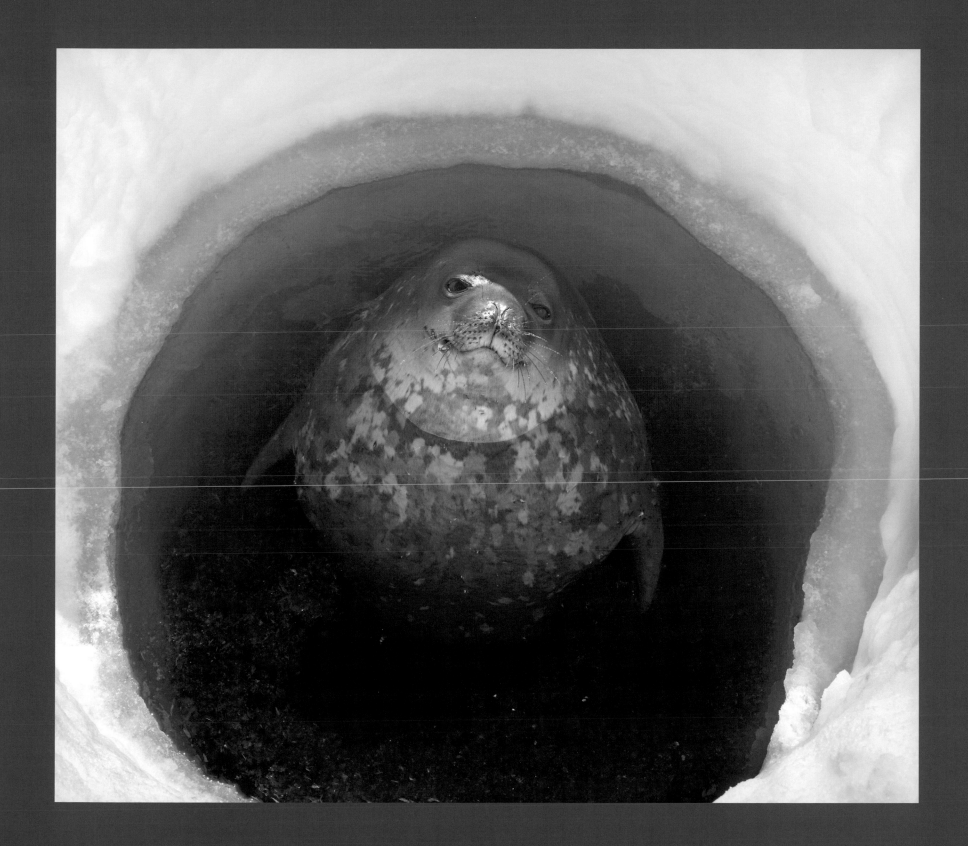

Seals Have Personalities Too

Bearded, Hooded, Harp, Ringed and Ribbon in the north, and Elly, Crabby, Furry, Ross, Lep and Wedd in the south. No, not teams of solicitors but polar seals. Eleven in total, and I've been in the water with nine of them.

They have the poles in common, but each species has its own unique character. I can speak for all of them except the Ross and the Ribbon; the former I've seen only twice, and the latter lives in the Sea of Okhotsk. Yes, I too had to check where that is. It's the area south of the Bering Strait, between Alaska to the east and Japan and Russia to the west.

Leopard seals give me the biggest buzz. Like polar bears, they're large, sexy, charismatic, intelligent hunters. If you'd asked me ten years ago if they posed a threat to divers, I'd have said no, but then one dragged the scientist Kirsty Brown under water and drowned her. It was obviously an attack in the way that leps have been seen taking on young elephant seals, but Kirsty was terribly unlucky. The seal must have known almost immediately that she wasn't prey, but it held her down for a fatally long time.

A lep's normal prey is, surprisingly, krill, though we usually film them when they're in the mood to take penguins. They hang around the rookeries in summer, picking off the adults and youngsters. Their big, long flippers make them very manoeuvrable so they can chase and catch the penguins in open water. But they also lie in the surf zone, ▶

Swimming lesson. A Weddell pup learns to swim at
about a month old. On its first under-ice dip, it stays
close to mum and doesn't go far from its breathing hole.

Previous page
Fellow diver. This Weddell popped up in a dive hole we had
drilled only an hour earlier.

▶ waiting for a penguin to come close enough to grab. They'll usually tolerate divers, though they may show their annoyance by making threat displays in front of your lens. They open their jaws in a huge gape. I've had one take the whole of the front of the camera in its mouth. I could hear its teeth scratching on the metal and could, in all honesty, have focused in on the seal's tonsils.

Leps don't have an equivalent in the Arctic. None of the seals in the north prey on anything apart from fish or krill. The most numerous is the ringed seal, the staple food of polar bears. That probably accounts for its ultra-wary behaviour; it's very hard to film. You never see one under water, only on the surface, no more than a few metres from an escape hole that it can use to slip quickly back into the water. A ringed seal sleeps on the ice, but only for short spells. Every 20 seconds, it will raise its head to look around.

Ringed seal pups are born in lairs under the snow, hidden from view. But a polar bear can smell one from up to a mile away if the wind is right. It will zero in on the invisible seal and then smash down through the snow roof of the lair to grab the seal before it escapes through its hole into the water. Maybe one in twenty attempts is successful.

A ringed seal can live under solid ice. It keeps it breathing holes open by rasping at the edges with its sharp claws. The Weddell seal in the Antarctic has the same fast-ice habitat, but it keeps its holes open ▶

Whitecoat. A harp pup at a week old must be one of the cutest animals on the planet. But in the Gulf of St Lawrence, its white coat is what the sealers are after when they take to the ice for the annual hunt.

▶ with its front incisor teeth, moving its head from side to side and pulling down at the same time. You can make a good guess at the age of a Wedd from the wear on its teeth. I think these are the most handsome of the southern seals, with a gentle, docile nature that makes me think of a dog. We used to tag the pups, sleeping so soundly next to mum that neither of them would wake even as we crept in, spread the tail flipper and clipped on the metal tag.

The most likely seal to bite a diver? A southern fur seal, without a doubt. Once thought to be extinct because of the degree to which fur seals were hunted for their pelts, they're now back with a vengeance. In fact, there may be more of them now than when they were first discovered in the early 1800s.

They're good fun to dive with, especially when they're in socialising groups in the late afternoon. They play a sort of underwater king of the castle, when one will take up position on a half-submerged rock, and the others try to displace it by swimming in fast and taking nips at its flippers. They're remarkably agile, with a spine so flexible they could easily bite their own tails if they wanted. Being accepted as a member of an animal group is the ultimate accolade for a wildlife photographer, though what's a mere nip to a furry is a serious puncture wound in your drysuit or even your elbow. So being in their presence can be a mixed blessing.

Only one other seal has actually bitten me, and that was in the Gulf of St Lawrence. The visibility under the ice was fairly murky. ▶

Get lost! Southern fur seals sometimes want to simply
test your nerve, zooming in at high speed, jaws agape –
here swimming among kelp off South Georgia.

▶ I was hanging around hoping for a glimpse of some male harp seals that I knew were close. I could hear their whistles all around me. Suddenly a seal shot out of the gloom straight for me. I just had time to stick the camera up as defence before I felt a sharp pain, as if someone had stuck a needle into the base of my thumb. Blood oozed into the water. Mum had decided I was too close to her breathing hole when her pup was on top of the ice. In fact, I could see the wee one peering down as I beat a retreat.

Harps and northern bearded seals both like to live in loose pack ice. The bearded is a bigger animal, much prized by Inuit hunters for its skin. They cut it into long, thin strips to use for lashing down anything they want to carry on their sledges. It's remarkably strong yet stretchy, a sort of natural bungee cord.

In temperament, the bearded is almost like the Wedd, often easy-going if you move in slowly. But seals in the Arctic are never as trusting as down south. Polar bears make sure of that.

The commonest seal, indeed some reckon the most abundant large mammal in the world, is the crabeater. Another pack-ice seal, it could number as many as 20 million around the Antarctic.

Crabeaters slither around on the floes, jaws and nostrils dripping with pale brown, salivary mucus, making a sort of viscous, bad-tempered, snuffling sound. Perhaps "crabbie by name, crabbie by nature" sums up its character. Despite its numbers, we still don't know a great deal ▶

Bad breath. Seal mouths are full of nasty bacteria. A bite often leads to secondary infections. Not pleasant.

▶ about the crabeater. Even its name is a misnomer, since it doesn't actually eat crabs. British sailors might have heard the Norwegian sealers refer to it as eating 'krips', a generic Norwegian word meaning small crustacean. And the wrong name stuck.

On the other hand, there's nothing confusing about why the elephant seal picked up its name. Its size and massive nose make it unmistakable.

Strange how the biggest of the seals should be the most timid in the water. When they go to sea, they either spend time in the murky shallows just off the beach or head straight out into open water. If I did manage to get one in the viewfinder, it paid to leave it plenty of panic room. If the seal felt cornered, it would make its escape right over you.

There's a flippers-down winner for the strangest polar seal: a male hooded seal. At first glance, this Arctic character looks a bit like the ellies down south, but its big nose is even more spectacular. When a male wants to show his dominance, he'll inflate his wrinkled proboscis until it covers the front of his face and half his head. But when truly aroused, a small, fleshy balloon begins to appear from one nostril. It starts the size of a tennis ball and grows to a football until, finally, it's more like a glorious bright red beach ball. It dangles out of his nose, and he shakes it furiously in the direction of his rival. You can't help laughing when you see two males shaping up for a fight, their nasal displays out in all their glory. ■

Seal company. These elephant seals seem to be
deriving great pleasure from each other's
close company. It's written all over their faces.

Top left
Going … Once the leopard seal has the penguin in its jaws,
there's little chance of escape.
Top right
Going… The lep starts to flay its prey, holding the penguin by
its skin and shaking it.
Above
Gone.

Above
Not-so-happy feet. The first filming and photography of
leopard seals under water was when we recorded them at
Dream Island for *Life in the Freezer*.

Close-up. In the company of a cameraman, a lep is curious
and confident. I suspect that it sees itself reflected in the
curved dome of the camera lens and starts displaying to
what it thinks is another seal.

Old man of the sea. The bearded seal's long, sensitive whiskers act as feelers to help it locate molluscs and other prey on the muddy seafloor.

Hoodie. When his nasal sac is fully inflated, a male hooded seal is unmistakable. It makes the weirdest sound, too – imagine a cowbell with electronic overtones.

A Stinker Eats

We call it a geep, pronounced like the four-wheel-drive car. Giant petrel, initials GP – it's obvious really. The sealers and whalers called it 'stinker' for another good reason. It's a scavenger par excellence, and it must have flourished wherever seals and whales were slaughtered.

This one is eating a dead fur seal. There are plenty of them on the beach after the breeding season – especially old male seals, who have exhausted themselves defending their harems of females while mating with as many of them as possible. There are worse ways to die, I suppose.

When disturbed, a geep can summon the defence that all petrels have, regurgitating foul-smelling oil from their stomachs, projectile vomiting it with great accuracy and an extra flick of the head over anything within a metre or so.

We used to ring several hundred geeps every year on Signy, and it wasn't just the birds that were called 'stinkers' after a day's work.

Gold Harbour, South Georgia, January, filming for *The Blue Planet*, BBC.

Good Old Adélies

We have a saying among film-makers that penguins may be birds, but they're actually honorary mammals – in terms of being great subjects for wildlife programmes. And while I have the biggest admiration for the solid, no-nonsense toughness of the male emperors and their winter vigil with their eggs, I keep my biggest affection for the feisty little Adélies. They come top of the bill.

On Signy, when they began to return to their rookeries in September, I really felt that spring had arrived. They'd find their same nest sites from the year before and then defend them until their partners from the previous season turned up. Their breeding cycle takes a shade over three months from copulation to egg-laying, incubation, hatching, feeding and fledging. I always had a huge buzz simply sitting beside the colony with a long lens, looking for little intimate details of their behaviour.

This Adélie chick is almost fully fledged, trying for what could be its final meal from a parent before it's left to fend for itself. Any second now, the adult will regurgitate a mouthful of krill from its stomach, tilt its head to its chick with beak gaping, and one more link in the food chain will be forged. The chick is easily recognised as such by its white chin. It'll be a year before it will have adult coloration. Climate change and lack of food may prevent it ever reaching that stage.

Fish Islands, Antarctic Peninsula, February, filming for *Frozen Planet*, BBC.

Know Your Bear

You have to work with a great field assistant if you're going to be successful with filming polar bears, and Jason Roberts is one of the best.

Even with the longest lenses on the camera, I need to be about 50 metres from the bear to get the close-ups for a good sequence. We drive around, frequently stopping to look through binoculars, heading into any wind so our sound and smell won't carry in the animal's direction. When we see a bear, we slow down, trying to keep the snow-machine revs low and steady, driving one behind the other so as to look as small and unthreatening as possible to the bear. A bear's eyesight and hearing is about as acute as a human's.

We might spend an hour or more slowly working our way in close to about 100 metres away. Often the bear will be too wary to hang around. He'll lift his head, see us, turn and walk away. No point in following. Bears need undisturbed space before they'll start behaving naturally.

But in time we'll find one who's hunting but still lets us and the snow machines within 100 metres or so. I give him another 15 minutes to make sure he's settled. Then I quietly prepare the camera gear and walk slowly towards the bear, hoping to make the magic 50-metre distance for the wides and close-ups. All animals like their personal space, and in the case of bears, I reckon it's about 25-35 metres. Stay outside that, and it may well not be bothered by your presence. But every bear is an individual, and so you can't always be sure.

Bears can run very fast, up to 40kph, but usually not very far, less than 50 metres. So I also know that if he is going to come at me, he's going to give me some warning. He'll start with a slow walk in my direction.

But I'm confident I can keep filming even as a bear starts towards me, because back at the snow machines, Jason is also concentrating on the bear. And when its attention turns too much to me, he'll start the machine and give it lots of throttle, so that as he whizzes by me, he frightens away the advancing bear.

Yes I know what you're thinking: lots of trust between Jason and me. It's all worked so far, and I wouldn't be writing this if it hadn't.

Leifdefjord, Svalbard, Norwegian Arctic, April, filming for *The Life of Mammals*, BBC.

Mind-reading by Pawprint

Sometimes you can tell from a polar bear's pawprints what's going on in his mind. These steps alongside this crack in the ice show that the bear is hunting. He knows that seals use these cracks, and he pads quietly along the edge, looking for the *aglu*, the tiny hole in the thin ice where the seal has stuck its nose up for air between dives.

If he finds such a hole, the bear will go into hunting mode, waiting and listening for the return of the seal. He knows the slightest sound of his feet on the ice will carry into the water and warn the seal. So he may stand there motionless for hours. But as soon as he hears the tiny slap of water ripples in the hole, his body stiffens into alertness. The seal is just below, about to surface for air. When there is a sharp exhalation of seal breath at the hole, the bear rises on his hind legs to smash down through the ice and grab his prey.

Leifdefjord, Svalbard, Norwegian Arctic, May, filming for *Extreme Animals*, BBC.

Bonding of the Wanderers

I was trying to film very young wandering albatross chicks being fed, but we'd arrived a few days early and they hadn't yet hatched. But up on the hill crests, adults were displaying – magnificent males with their 3-metre wingspan, beaks raised to the heavens, completely engrossed in their courting. I was able to crawl on hands and knees in the gullies between the raised clumps of tussock grass until eventually I was lying on my belly right underneath their outstretched wings. The birds weren't bothered in the slightest, and my most vivid memory is actually of the sloppy slap of their big webbed feet as they padded around in the gloopy, muddy grass.

Bird Island, South Georgia, Antarctica, March, filming for *The Blue Planet*, BBC.

Misfortune Feeds the Fox

Cold, starvation, thin ice and polar bears are all challenges for Arctic animals. On top of all those more normal hazards, caribou can have the sheer bad luck to be caught in an avalanche. This one had perhaps been scratching for lichen on the scree when the snow cornice above collapsed, leaving no chance of escape.

The milder spring temperatures were just thawing the corpse enough for this Arctic fox to keep returning for a few scraps of food. I sat quietly, and the fox was completely unbothered by my presence.

I do have a soft spot for Arctic foxes. When we live in the cabins of Svalbard on a filming trip, it's never too long before one turns up, darting around and investigating the sledge and anything on it. You feel as if you've been adopted by a friendly stray dog. Foxes' tracks can be everywhere out on the sea ice. Arctic foxes are said to follow polar bear tracks to find old polar bear kills. They can also dig down into seal lairs to attack and kill the young ringed seal pups.

Fitting tags to them has shown they may cover remarkable distances every day while foraging for food, upwards of 80 kilometres. One fox in north Baffin Island wandered more than 240 kilometres from its den in winter but was back in its home territory for the following summer.

I had the chance to hold one briefly while I was filming with a scientist. Its body weighed almost nothing, a shade over 3 kilos, and I marvelled at how efficient its fur must be to let such a small animal expend so much energy yet stay warm in the brutal conditions of winter.

Bellsund, Svalbard, April, filming for *Planet Earth*, BBC.

Happy Birthday Belugas

If polar bears epitomise the Arctic ice, then belugas for me are the spirits of the northern seas. Pure white, pure curiosity. You find these whales all through the Canadian Arctic, but the best time and place to film them is at the north end of Baffin Island in the late spring. In early June, there's a short period of clear water between the ice clearing and the green plankton bloom starting. That's when to try for the belugas.

The sounds of a pod's exhalations carries miles in still air. On calm nights, we'd hear the whales long before we saw them. They often followed the edge of the ice, where open water met the fast ice that covered the bays and inlets. As they swam closer, it was usually a matter of simply slipping into the water, and they would come over for a look. I turned myself into an object of their curiosity by singing down my snorkel as I looked into the depths. "Happy Birthday" was pretty effective, I'm sure that brought them in closer.

They'd appear as white shapes below me, swimming on their backs, looking up at my silhouette against the water's surface. All around I could hear them chirping, squeaking and whistling. No wonder they're called canaries of the sea.

These belugas were with me in open water, but they also frequently venture under heavy pack ice, when the sea surface is almost 100 per cent covered with large ice floes. That's an impressive feat for an air-breathing mammal, and not without risk, because it will drown if it doesn't find cracks in the ice where it can surface to breathe.

One pair of scientists fastened recorders to belugas that measured the time and depth of their dives. They found that when under heavy, lumpy, jumbled ice, the belugas made V-shaped dives in between surfacings. It seems they went deep, then used their sonar or their sight to look ahead for the next place they could come up for air.

Lancaster Sound, Canadian Arctic, June, filming for *Life at the Edge*, National Geographic.

Ellie with a Fetish

Ellies don't particularly like ice – they're much more seals of the sub-Antarctic than the true polar species such as crabeaters and Weddells. This big male is showing off the inflatable proboscis that gave elephant seals their name. When they roar their loudest, hauled out on their beach, the noise is clearly audible a kilometre or so away. It sounds like a cross between a belch and a fart.

I took this shot just off the jetty at Signy. The seal was roaring in defiance, because we'd just run towards him waving and shouting. He had been lumbering up the slipway, looking as if he was intent on snuggling up to our inflatable boat lying against the boat shed.

We always had a few ellies every summer who took a fetishist's delight in rubbing against the rubber pontoons of the Zodiac. One actually managed to roll its entire body into the boat itself, his head hanging over the bow and his flippers tucked in next to the anchor. We had a hell of a job persuading him out without destroying the entire boat and the outboard that was still on the stern.

Borge Bay, Signy Island, South Orkney Islands, Antarctica, December.

Happy as Seals in Mud

Ellies on shore in summer – big, smelly, runny-nosed, rheumy-eyed, skin-peeling, farting pods of seals. They look like the tables in a rundown fleapit of a snooker hall, with scabby tufts of curling baize peeling off them. Lying together in heaps, either fast asleep or belching and roaring grumpily, they suffer each other's company to conserve body heat during this period of moulting. Muddy wallows are perfect for them, some say to alleviate the itchiness they feel at this time of their year.

When the moult is complete, the ellies go back to sea. Then they're transformed. These truly marine animals can find their way across 1000 kilometres of open sea to specific feeding grounds – where for weeks on end, they'll dive continuously, spending up to 55 minutes of every hour under water at a depth of 1200 metres or more.

They're capable of catching fish in total darkness; indeed, some perfectly healthy ellies are completely blind. Their sensitive whiskers can detect the minute pressure differences left in the wake of a swimming fish, and they can follow its 'track' through the water.

On some dives, their descent dramatically slows. The seals flutter like leaves as they drift slowly downwards. The suspicion is that they're actually sleeping during these drifts, safer from predators down there than they would be at the surface.

St Andrew's Bay, South Georgia, February, filming for *Life in the Freezer*, BBC.

Igloo Architecture

Sue and I were making a programme about an Inuit family we know well from northern Baffin Island. Andrew Taqtu and his son Apak were out on the sea ice filming with us, and part of the story involved Apak helping his dad build an igloo. It's still a crucial survival skill for a person aspiring to be a guide, and when an igloo's finished, it's much more wind- and storm-proof than most tents.

The key is to choose the right kind of snow. You need dense windpack that can be cut into blocks with a snow-saw or knife. The blocks should be slightly curved, so that they naturally make the igloo circular. The Inuit place one block next to another but work upwards, not as a series of level walls as you or I would lay bricks in a house but in a spiral, with each block getting bigger. They also keep the middle of the block above so that it bridges the gap between the blocks below so there are no continuous lines of weakness in the structure.

The whole thing can be built by one man. After the dome is finished, he goes outside and uses his knife to scoop snow, pressing it into the cracks to keep out the wind. A skilled man can build an igloo in 45 minutes.

The *qamatiq* in the foreground was made from wood, built to be as light as possible. Some driftwood comes ashore on Arctic islands after being carried down big rivers such as the Mackenzie, but the ingenious Inuit originally used many different parts of animals for their sledges. The makers of the very old *qamatiqs* split frozen Arctic char (a fish like a salmon) lengthways and then laid them end-to-end. They wrapped the long bundles of fish in seal hides, binding them together with rope made from the skin of bearded seals. That made the runners. Pieces of bone or antler were lashed to each runner to keep them parallel, and then a smooth running surface was created by adding a glaze of ice to the sealskin with a handful of wet moss or simply by urinating on it.

I always see this image as an advert along the lines of 'Wherever you are, Cozyglo Heating will keep out the winter chill'. Or in this case, 'Cozyglo Seal Blubber Lamp'. So that's probably why I usually stick to pictures and seldom do words.

Cape Crauford, Lancaster Sound, Canadian Arctic, March, filming *A Boy Among Polar Bears* for the BBC.

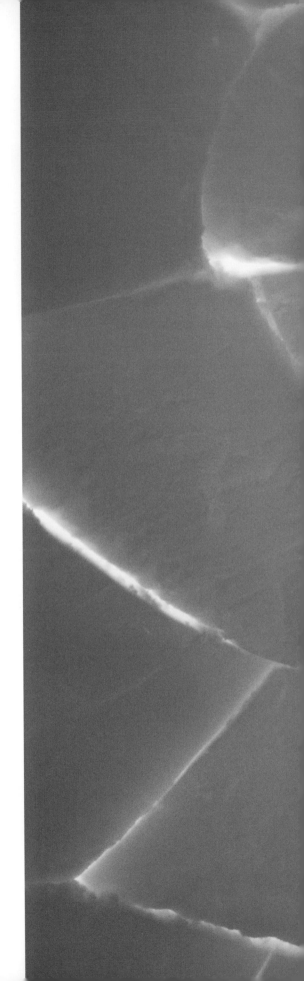

Igloos and Glasses

Shooyuk here was putting the finishing touches to the inside of an igloo he'd just built. He was shaving off the edges of the keystone final piece of ice so it fitted perfectly. But he kept cursing at his glasses being covered by the chips of ice that were raining down. As I listened to his good-natured grumbling, I remembered a story told to me by Andrew Taqtu, another Inuit guide friend of mine, who also wore glasses.

Andrew was out hunting seals on the sea ice in spring. He'd stopped for a brew in some rough ice, with rather restricted views around him in terms of being able to see bears from far away. Ten minutes later, with the tea just on the boil, a young polar bear suddenly appeared from behind a lump of pack ice and made for him. Andrew rushed to the box on the back of the sledge for his rifle. Lifting it out, he turned to find the bear very, *very* close. "Suddenly I couldn't see anything. The bear's breath had fogged up my glasses," he told me. I think he swung out with the rifle, catching the bear on the nose, and it ran away.

He tells the story now as a joke against himself, and as proof of one of the classically wise Inuit sayings: "It's not the bear you can see that's going to get you."

Lancaster Sound, April, filming for *Arctic Kingdom – Life at the Edge*, National Geographic.

Being Like a Bear

The Inuit elders told me, "If you want to learn to hunt seals, you must watch *nanuq*."

Experienced seal hunters such as Andrew certainly use just the same skills as polar bears. In front of him he's cleared away some of the slush from the tiny breathing hole in the young ice. Like a bear, Andrew is waiting – 'still hunting', they call it – absolutely quiet, eyes fixed on that hole, alert for the seal's return. His hands are inside sealskin mitts, his boots are soled with hide from the bearded seal. They'll keep him warm with no need to shuffle or wriggle his toes. Silence and patience are the keys.

Lancaster Sound, Canadian Arctic, March, filming for *A Boy Among Polar Bears*, BBC.

Bird-snatching

This was eye-and-hand coordination so deft that I could barely follow the action with a camera. The Inuit choose their hunting points along the cliffs where millions of little auks come every summer to breed. They wait semi-concealed behind little walls that might have been built last year or 500 years ago; there's no way to tell – the birds and the hunters have been coming here for a long, long time.

The little auks sit on their ledges, but they're ready for mobbing behaviour whenever gulls or gyrfalcons fly overhead. The great flock takes off, climbs to intercept the intruder and gives it a hard time. Then all the birds circle once or twice before landing. Having seen off one hunter, it's then they may fall prey to the other. As the birds fly past his blind, the Inuk thrusts his pole out at full length, whipping it through the air parallel with and just below the flying birds. Then in a split second he twists it into the vertical position so that the birds effectively fly into the net. Here he's about to catch two birds at once.

An experienced hunter can catch 300-400 auks in an afternoon. The dead birds are left to cool for 24 hours before the next stage in preparing the delicacy *kiviaq*. The hunter first stuffs the carcasses, 300 or more of them, into a bag made of sealskin. He sews this up tight, smears the stitching with rancid fat to keep the flies from laying their eggs on it and then leaves it under a pile of very heavy stones.

The carcasses rot in the airless sack for six months and are then eaten raw with the feathers pulled off. I was told it tasted like very ripe cheese. I took the locals' word for it.

Siorapaluk, Greenland, July, filming for *Human Planet*, BBC.

The Patience of the Bear-spotter

I've seen an Inuit stand on a piece of ice like this for almost two hours at -25°C, with 10 knots of wind and the sun sliding around barely above the horizon. He just slowly, very slowly, scans the horizon, steadying the telescope against the shaft of the ice spear that he uses to test the sea-ice thickness. He is seemingly impervious to the numbing cold, with his caribou parka and pants and sealskin mukluk boots.

It's the best way to find polar bears, which are more active in the cool of the night than during the full sun of the day. But unless they're moving, boy are they hard to see – especially in rough ice, at a mile away, half-hidden behind the lumps and distorted by the miraging cold air that turns everything into a shimmering illusion. It needs 100 per cent concentration and practised eyes to pick one out.

So he minutely studies the ice, looking for a piece that's maybe not quite the same as it was when he looked a few minutes ago, a shape that's a different shade of white – any clue to pick out our quarry.

And me, I just realise again that without these people I'm a southern film-maker who on his own would have no chance of coming back with any bear footage.

Lancaster Sound, Canadian Arctic, March, filming for *Arctic Kingdom – Life at the Edge*, National Geographic.

Life, Death and Hypocrisy

I'll offer two points of view for this picture.

It's disturbing isn't it, the juxtaposition of the smiling youngster with the decapitated head of a narwhal? The son and his father had just eaten some *muktuk* (narwhal blubber) together. Both boy and man seemed to share pride in the skill and experience the father had shown to land the whale. Listening to him talking quietly to his son, I felt how the best Inuit hunters do indeed have a deep affinity with the sea, the ice and the animals. It gives them a wisdom, understanding and appreciation of their environment that more 'developed' people have long since lost.

Is it being hypocritical to claim to be a conservationist on the one hand but also a supporter of some native hunting on the other? So much of an Inuit's identity is wrapped up in his traditional knowledge of his land that I've seen a man transformed from an apparently indolent member of the village community to someone sounding and looking truly alive when he takes his dogs or his snow machine out onto the spring sea ice.

When a hunt is successful, the hunter won't boast about his prowess but rather how his behaviour and respect for his prey meant the animal offered itself to him. I've recognised how that translates into the way the Inuit use as much of the animal as they can.

It could be seen as the thin end of a morally dubious wedge when we with our lives feel we can impose our beliefs on others from very different cultures. Saving some animals may hasten the end of a cultural way of life. We do have to think carefully about our own practices before banning what we find offensive in others. It's our emissions that are stressing and screwing the Inuit's environment; how many CO_2-derived pleasures would you give up in exchange for him stopping hunting?

But when the truth is faced, few Inuit are as good hunters as this boy's father. Too many are poor shots. They go for the narwhal but all too often they miss. The wounded animal isn't caught and brought to shore, but swims away to die elsewhere, an uncounted exception to the hunting quota that applies to that community. This is a terrible wastage, even if overall numbers of narwhal returning each year to some communities do seem to be remaining steady.

In 2010 the Canadian government banned the international export of narwhal tusks from 17 communities in Nunavut because their local populations were considered to be at risk of overhunting, or as a precautionary measure until more population data was gathered.

Admiralty Inlet, Lancaster Sound, Canadian Arctic, June.

Emperors of Ice

2 April: The Emps Gather

Only last month the sea was surging round the base of the ice cliffs. Now everywhere is frozen solid. The first of the emperors are returning. How do these penguins do it – travelling from hundreds of miles away in the ice-strewn sea back to the same place every year – especially when that place changes from year to year? This is not like a static rookery on an island. Here icebergs calve from the front of this ice shelf, completely altering its appearance if a big-enough piece breaks off. Yet every year the penguins are back.

We cut steps down a snow ramp to the ice, where we can see the penguins strung out in a line to the north. Some stand in groups, with odd birds wandering around, seeking their mates. Occasionally one stops, ducks its head, draws its shoulders back and utters a trumpeting call. Every hour dozens more penguins toboggan in on their bellies to join the colony.

I hadn't appreciated just how tall they were until I crouched next to one – we were easily eye to eye. Normally I avoid anthropomorphic descriptions, but these birds clearly possess a dignity, all the more pronounced because of their bulk. They walk with a regal gait, measured and slow, their heads dipping from side to side.

29 April: Huddling

It's bitterly cold today at the colony, -27°C, with 15 knots of wind. The emps are now huddling together in large groups of several hundred birds, those on the outside presenting an unbroken serried row of backs to the wind. The snow around each group is stained dirty green by their excrement – incongruously grass-like. The colour comes from salts in their bile, a sure sign that some are no longer digesting food ▶

The emperors return. Well provisioned with fat and with full bellies, the penguins walk back to the ice rookery.

▶ and are beginning their long fast, which will carry them through the even more fearsome cold to come.

Driven by the mechanics of huddling, entire groups slowly move across the snow. Birds on the outside push towards the warm middle, so they displace others and make the huddle creep like an amoeba. They are in search of mates, and the odd penguin occasionally detaches itself and sets off, calling, towards another group. Now and then an entire huddle breaks up, the warm air from bodies and breath hanging briefly above in a misty cloud.

For emps, conservation of energy is crucial. The males, which have already spent several weeks at the rookery, still have at least another three months to go without feeding – including 60 days of virtually complete darkness, when blizzard conditions can depress the windchill temperature to 100 degrees below zero.

I was bending over the camera, adjusting the lens, when a sniffly drop escaped from my long-suffering nose and fell straight onto the shutter-release button. It froze instantly and locked the camera until I returned to the warmth of the base. A frustrating end to the colony visit.

18 May: Mating

We watched two emps mating. Like the few other occasions when we'd witnessed the act, the pair were out on their own, away from any large groups. We kept our distance, knowing they would be easily disturbed, and stood in the freezing cold – we who had chosen to live in a tiny colony of all-male humans for an entire year – and felt only the slightest jealousy.

Despite the adverse circumstances, or perhaps because of them, the mating seems to me to be remarkably placid. Even the inevitable ▶

Egg-sitters. The males are still on duty but basking in the rays of the returning sun.

▶ love triangles are resolved without much fuss – a few seconds' biffing of flippers is enough to make one of the birds back down. The behaviour looks almost half-hearted, especially when I remember the keen aggression I've seen further north with chinstraps or Adélies.

16 July: New Dawning

I'm beginning to see light for the first time in six weeks. My eyes no longer need to strain for dim shapes, and there's colour and a feeling of distance being restored to the world. I'm anticipating the days when it won't take an hour to start the vehicle to come down here, when I might dare to handle the bare metal of a camera without gloves, when I can walk without stumbling over unseen lumps of ice.

I can just about make out some penguin silhouettes against the skyline, but there are no stars overhead, and I suppose it must be overcast. Though there's no wind, the sheer gloominess is very hostile.

All the females have long since left. It's only the males that are here, each with his precious egg on his feet. The males do the entire 60 days of incubation, while the females head for holes in the ice where they can dive and feed. I wonder how far they've had to go to find that open water. It can be anywhere from 30 to 150 kilometres.

29 July: Counting Penguins

Despite the gloomy conditions, we managed to make a pretty accurate guesstimate of the size of the colony today. A cold wind made the birds stand shoulder to shoulder in a tight teardrop-shaped huddle. We paced off the area and multiplied by the number of penguins per square metre. It came to just over 12,000 individuals. So with none of the females back yet, that would make this rookery number about 25,000 birds. It's one of the bigger ones in Antarctica. ▶

Mother's baby. Protected by the brood pouch, a baby is now looked after by its mother. It's starving father has left the rookery to feed up at sea.

▶ 15 August: Still incubating

Just over one glorious hour with the sun above the horizon, but bitterly cold, despite the lack of wind. Still lots of emps incubating. They shuffle slowly with their precious eggs balanced on their feet, tucked in their brood pouches. This bare patch of skin between their legs keeps the egg warm by direct contact with body heat. A male looks as if he has a wee pregnancy bump just above his feet, where the feathery flap covers the egg, protecting it from the chilling wind.

21 August: Chicks hatching

Today was the first chance to catch a glimpse of some of the chicks. I heard the high-pitched whistley cheeps as I walked towards the colony, but it took a while before I finally saw one peeking out from its parent's feet. Some of the very recently hatched chicks still had little white scraps of egg-tooth adhering to the ends of their beaks (used to chip their way out of the egg). Until the chicks are about ten days old, they remain well hidden under the parents' abdominal pouches. But as their downy feathers thicken, they're more able to maintain their own body heat and so reveal more of themselves.

I feel as though we've turned the corner of the year. There's a steady trickle of females still coming in over the sea ice, presumably those whose eggs have yet to hatch. It's one of the miracles of nature that a female penguin lays her egg and then returns two months later to refind her partner just as the egg is hatching. Though the male has the means to feed the chick for a few days, from a protein secretion he can produce in his crop, it's crucial for the long-term survival of the chick that the female makes a synchronous return. Only she has sufficient food for the first weeks of her chick's growth. ▶

Nursery feet. Now out of the pouch, the chicks are
growing fast on a diet of regurgitated seafood.

▶ **24 September: Chicks out and about**

There's quite a range of size now among the chicks. Some are still quite small. Their parents stand face to face, heads cocked, rocking backwards on their heels and seeming to show off their wobbly-headed chicks, which are still perched on their carers' horny feet. But other chicks are already too big for the pouch and show increasing independence. They scurry around like clockwork toys from adult to adult, eliciting food by repeatedly throwing back their heads and letting out their loud, whistling calls. They look to be torn by two forces – hunger and cold. When hunger overtakes the chill, they go begging. When they're chilled but not hungry, they huddle as the adults did over the winter.

12 October: Sheltering from the wind

It was freezing cold today, but you'd never know from the photographs. We had a full-on blizzard a few days before, and there's still 25 knots of gusting wind up on top of the ice shelf. But many of the emps have moved in from the exposed area of the sea ice to cluster at the head of a natural creek between the ice cliffs.

It must be quite sheltered down there. The birds aren't huddling together for warmth, and the odd very small chick is out on its own, away from the shelter of its parent's feet. You can tell the birds have been here at the head of the creek for a while. The snow is dirtied with their faeces.

15 November: Returning from feeding

The birds returning from feeding are in magnificent condition. The golden sheen of their breast feathers merges with the deep orange ▶

Spring huddle. When times are cold and parents are away feeding,
the chicks huddle to keep warm, just as their fathers did in winter.

▶ of their necks, and their tapering beaks are tinted with a delicate shade of purple. All the while, the ice is breaking back towards the colony, allowing the adults to come and go with food more frequently.

Only a mile or so further out we can see wraiths of grey-black frost-smoke spiralling up against the fading orange sky – an indication of open water, where arriving penguins give up swimming and start tobogganing. Long shadows from the ice cliffs stretch over the emps. They are still calling through the deepening gloom as we draw away from them.

1 December: End of the colony

The time is approaching when the ice at the colony is going to break up. I can see open water only a few hundred metres from the ice cliffs. Already a few of the more advanced chicks are standing out there, ready to go swimming for the first time. The rest will follow very soon. It's a quiet, pastel evening, the quality of light uniquely Antarctic – clear as glass away to the bergs that are standing up against a grey sky. I'm filled with the old sense of privilege at having had the chance to see the emps right through their wonderful breeding cycle. I can almost forget the numbed fingers and toes of the past eight months. Almost, but not quite.

16 December: Departure

The ice and the emperors have gone.

Brunt Ice Shelf and Cape Washington, Antarctica, winter/spring, working for the British Antarctic Survey and later filming for *The Blue Planet*, BBC.

Emperor gathering. The chicks are nearly fledged and the ice is melting. In a matter of weeks, both will be gone.

Points North

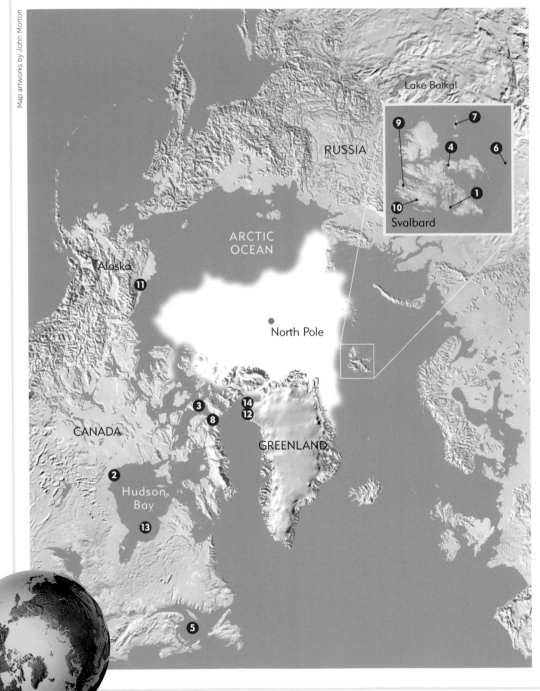

Map artworks by John Morton

Lake Baikal

RUSSIA

ARCTIC
OCEAN

Alaska

North Pole

CANADA

Hudson
Bay

GREENLAND

Svalbard

The sea ice depicts very approximate
ice cover in September

Points South

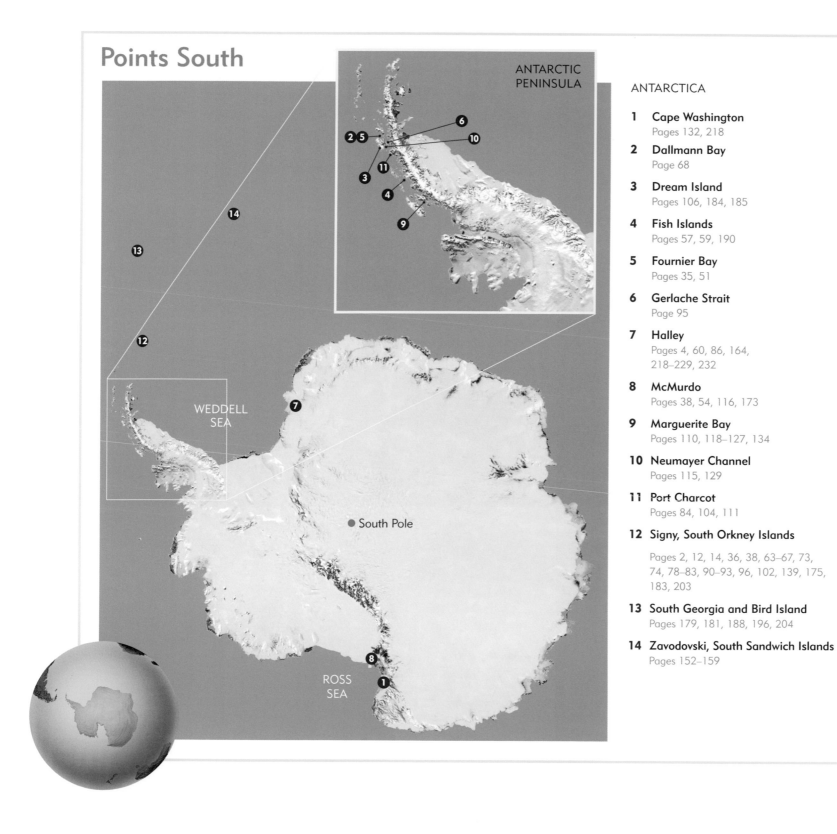

ANTARCTIC
PENINSULA

WEDDELL
SEA

● South Pole

ROSS
SEA

Acknowledgements

I owe big thanks to many people.

Sue Flood and I shared so many special moments before and after our time on the ice floe. She was a creative and energetic producer and these days shows even more vision as a photographer. She helped me through murky waters to a clearer understanding of many things. Thanks Sue.

Without Gordon Downie as a dive buddy, I wouldn't have enjoyed my first dives nearly as much as I did. Pete and Paula Vine made my early Red Sea trips special, and with any luck we'll continue to share seaborne adventures. Thanks P & P.

Bill Abernethy showed me sights in Scottish rivers I'd scarcely have believed. Cheers Bill.

It will have been obvious while you read this book that my time with BAS down south was hugely influential in my life. Sincere thanks go to all those with whom I spent summers and winters on BAS bases and ships. Your enthusiasm, support and FID humour helped me in all kinds of ways. You were all the best of companions. Special thanks go to Norman Cobley, Nick Cox, Paul Drummond, Dave Fletcher, Neil Gilbert, Stuart Lawrence, Rick Price, Dave Rootes and Greg Wilkinson.

Films are truly collaborative efforts. Researchers find the best information, producers make inspired and often brave decisions about which sequences to film, and programme managers and coordinators lay the complicated logistics in place so that I'm in the right place at the right time in front of the animals. Great editors find imaginative ways to cut around my shortcomings, and composers and dubbing mixers bring their talents to the sound mix. The eventual whole becomes much greater than the sum of the parts.

It's been my good fortune and privilege to work with many of the best camera and production people in the business – huge thanks to you all. Too many to mention individually but special thanks to David Attenborough, Jeffery Boswall, Mark Brownlow, Darren Flaxstone, Alastair Fothergill, Martha Holmes, Martin Hughes Games, Brian Leith, Steve Leonard, Patrick Morris, Sean Morris, Martin Pailthorpe, Karen Partridge,

Jo Payne, Brando Quilici and Dave Stewart. Your passion and enthusiasm, even if at times maddeningly misguided in the eyes of this cameraman, made the best programmes happen.

In the community of camerapersons, thanks to so many of you for your advice and support, especially Doug Anderson, Hilary and Alistair MacEwen, Hugh Miles, Mike Richards and Pete Scoones.

On location, tough shoots were all the more memorable by being in the company of good scientists and guides. My thanks to all of you who helped me bring back the images, particularly from the polar places – John Durban and Bob Pitman, Looty Pijamini, Jerome and Dion Poncet, Rob Robbins, Jason Roberts, Ian Stirling and Andrew Taqtu. Quark Expeditions took me to some new Antarctic locations, for which I'm very grateful; Paul and Jodie Allen did that too in real style. You are generous people, thank you.

For this book, Liam Allan was an early proofreader of some parts. The Hog dug deep for the motorbike information. David Helton came up with many of the short story titles that brought them to life. Stephen Johnson prepared the pictures for reproduction to his usual impeccable standards. Thanks to all of you.

Freeze Frame owes most to the two people who worked with me to bring it to reality. Huge thanks to Roz Kidman Cox for her always sensible and good-humoured editorial advice and experience. Long live the hyphen!

When I conceived this book I wanted it to be classy, elegant and friendly. Simon Bishop's design embodies those qualities with real flair. Thanks Simon.

And finally – I said to myself at the start of this final page that I wouldn't make this an Oscar-winning speech mentioning everyone who had ever touched me. But of course I want to close by saying thanks to my mother and father. Mum I'm sure would have offered her usual encouragement if she were still with us, and my thanks and love to Dad for deep-down, way-back inspiration as a self-made photographer himself.

It's been a blast.

Front cover: **Doug in the sidecar**
Nikon FE + 35mm Nikkor;
Kodachrome 64; 1/125 @ f11

Back cover: **Lunging humpbacks**
Nikon FE + 24mm Nikkor;
Kodachrome 200; 1/250 @ f8

Back-cover flap: **Doug and camera**
Nikon F90 + 80–200mm Nikkor;
Fuji Sensia 100; 1/250 @ f5.6

Front endpaper: **Iceberg and penguins**
Canon 1Ds Mk 2 + 100-400mm Canon;
200 ISO; 1/250 @ f8

Page 1: **Polar bears at sunset, Churchill**
Nikon F90 + 80-200mm Nikkor;
Fuji Sensia 200; 1/250 @ f5.6

Page 2: **Backlit climbers**
Nikon F2 + 24mm Nikkor;
Ektachrome 64; 1/250 @ f8

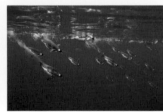

Page 4: **Emperors diving**
Nikonos 5 + 15mm Nikkor; Fuji Sensia
200 pushed to 400; 1/250 @ f5.6

Page 7: **David and Doug, Svalbard**
Nikon F90 + 24mm Nikkor;
Fuji Sensia 100; 1/250 @f8

Page 8: **Doug and the Arctic fox**
Nikon F90 + 20–40mm Tamron;
Fuji Sensia 100; 1/250 @ f8

Page 11: **Doug behind the Baikal
sledge hide** Nikon FE + 35mm Nikkor;
Kodachrome 64; 1/250 @ f11

Page 13: **Backlit drifting snow**
Nikon F2 + 80–200mm Nikkor;
Ektachrome 64; 1/250 @ f16

Page 14: **Sea ice, Signy**
Nikon F2 + 24mm Nikkor;
Ektachrome 64; 1/250 @ f11

Page 15: **A cold March day,
Kong Karl's Land** Canon G10; 100
ISO; 1/125 @ f11

Page 16: **Cabin door nameplate,
Kong Karl's Land** Canon G10; 200
ISO; 1/125 @ f11

Page 17: **Jason on the snow slope,
Kong Karl's Land** Canon G10;
200 ISO; 1/125 @ f8

Page 18: **The filming hut, Kong Karl's
Land** Canon G10; 100 ISO;
1/125 @ f11

Page 19: **Polar bear at the window,
Kong Karl's Land** Canon G10;
400 ISO; 1/30 @ f8

Page 19: **Doug and his scare guns,
Kong Karl's Land** Canon G10;100 ISO;
1/250 @ f8

Page 20: **Polar bear den, Kong Karl's
Land** Canon G10; 100 ISO;
1/250 @ f11

Page 21: **Doug in the snow-blind,
Kong Karl's Land** Canon G10; 100
ISO; 1/250 @ f11

Page 23: **Cubs at the den entrance**
Canon EOS 1 + 600mm Canon;
Fuji Sensia 100; 1/350 @ f8

Page 25: **Mum and her two cubs**
Canon EOS 1 + 100–400mm Canon;
Fuji Sensia 100; 1/250 @ f11

Page 26: **Mum and a single cub**
Canon EOS 1 + 600mm Canon;
Fuji Sensia 200; 1/400 @ f8

Page 27: **Doug in the den, Kong Karl's
Land** Canon G10; 200 ISO; 1/30
@ f11

Page 28: **Rombuk village**
Nikon F90 + 80–200mm Nikkor;
Fuji Sensia 100; 1/125 @ f11

Page 28: **Doug by his wee cave**
Nikon F90 + 20–40mm Tamron;
Fuji Sensia 100; 1/250 @ f11

Page 29: **Snow leopard footprints**
Nikon F90 + 20–40mm Tamron;
Fuji Sensia 100; 1/125 @ f5.6

Page 31: **Doug and the moose**
Nikon FE + 35mm Nikkor;
Kodachrome 64; 1/125 @ f8

Page 32: **Beluga spyhopping**
Nikon F90 + 80–200mm Nikkor;
Fuji Sensia 100; 1/500 @ f8

Page 33: **Belugas from above**
Nikon F90 + 80–200mm Nikkor;
Fuji Sensia 100; 1/500 @ f4

Page 35: **Humpbacks lunge-feeding**
See cover shot details

Page 36: **Doug with his old Bolex**
Nikon FE + 24mm Nikkor;
Kodachrome 64; 1/125 @ f8

Page 38: **Doug in the dive hole**
Canon 1DS Mk 2 + 17–40mm Canon;
100 ISO; 1/125 @ f8

Page 38: **Doug ready to dive**
Nikon F2 + 80–200mm Nikkor;
Ektachrome 64; 1/250 @ f11

Page 39: **Doug under the iceberg**
Nikonos 5 + 15mm Nikkor;
Fuji Sensia 200; 1/125 @ f5.6

Page 40: **Humpback with the boat**
Canon 1Ds Mk 2 + 17–40mm Canon;
Seacam housing; 200 ISO; 1/500 @ f8

Page 41: **Doug with the humpbacks**
Canon 1Ds Mk 2 + 17–40mm Canon;
Seacam housing; 200 ISO; 1/250 @ f5.6

Page 42: **Vertical humpbacks**
Canon 1Ds Mk 2 + 17–40mm Canon;
Seacam housing; 200 ISO; 1/125 @ f8

Page 43: **Humpback eyeing up Doug**
Canon 1Ds Mk 2 + 17–40mm Canon;
Seacam housing; 200 ISO; 1/250 @ f5.6

Page 45: **Humpback mother and calf**
Canon 1Ds Mk 2 + 17–40mm Canon;
Seacam housing; 200 ISO; 1/250 @ f5.6

Page 46: **Doug, Frances and the truck**
Nikon FE + 35mm Nikkor;
Kodachrome 64; 1/500 @ f5.6

Page 47: **Doug in the sidecar**
See cover

Page 48: **Doug behind the Baikal
sledge hide** See page 10

Page 49: **Baikal seal emerging**
Nikon FE + 80–200mm Nikkor;
Kodachrome 64; 1/250 @ f8

Page 49: **Baikal seals**
Nikon FE + 80–200mm Nikkor;
Kodachrome 64; 1/500 @ f5.6

Page 49: **Lake Baikal sponge forest**
Nikonos 3 + 15mm Nikkor lens; Subsea
150 flash; Ektachrome 200; 1/60 @ f5.6

Page 51: **Filming a humpback**
Canon EOS 1 + 17–35mm Canon;
Fuji Sensia 100; 1/125 @ f8

Page 52: **Resting polar bear**
Nikon F90 + 80–200mm Nikkor;
Fuji Sensia 100; 1/125 @ f8

Page 54: **Sleeping Weddell**
Canon 1DS Mk 2 + 100–400mm
Canon; 200 ISO; 1/250 @ f8

Page 57: **Adélie chicks being fed**
Nikon F90 + 80–200mm Nikkor;
Fuji Sensia 100; 1/250 @ f8

Page 59: **Sunset, Fish Islands**
Canon 1DS Mk 2 + 17–40mm Canon;
200 ISO; 1/250 @ f8

Page 61: **Aurora, Halley**
Nikon F2 + 18mm Nikkor; Ektachrome
200 pushed to 800; 30 secs @ f2.8

Page 63: **Parhelion circle**
Nikon F2 + 24mm Nikkor;
Ektachrome 64; 1/250 @ f8

Page 65: **Orange lenticular clouds**
Nikon FE + 24mm Nikkor;
Ektachrome 100; 1/125 @ f8

Page 67: **Crystal clouds** Nikon F2 +
80–200mm Nikkor; Ektachrome 64;
1/250 @ f5.6; polarising filter

Page 69: **Dallmann Bay**
Canon 1Ds Mk 2 + 17–40mm Canon;
100 ISO; 1/125 @ f8; polarising filter

Page 71: **Doug warm and comfortable**
Canon G10; 100 ISO; 1/125 @ f8

Page 73: **Raised footsteps**
Petriflex + 28mm Petriflex;
Ektachrome 64; 1/125 @ f11

Page 75: **Backlit drifting snow**
Nikon F2 + 24mm Nikkor;
Ektachrome 200; 1/250 @ f11

Page 76: **Curved icicles**
Nikon FE + 24mm Nikkor;
Kodachrome 64; 1/30 @ f5.6

Page 77: **Ice-cave refuge**
Nikon FE + 24mm Nikkor;
Kodachrome 64; 1/60 @ f4

Page 79: **Frost flowers**
Nikon F2 + 35mm Nikkor;
Ektachrome 200; 1/125 @ f8

Page 81: **Sticky porridge**
Nikon F2 + 24mm Nikkor;
Kodachrome 64; 1/250 @ f8

Page 83: **Beached ice block**
Nikon F2 + 24mm Nikkor; Ektachrome
100; 1/125 @ f11; polarising filter

Page 85: **The berg that turned** Nikon
F90 + 20–40mm Tamron; Kodachrome
64; 1/250 @ f8; polarising filter

Page 87: **Ice cliff face**
Nikon F2 + 80–200mm Nikkor;
Kodachrome 64; 1/250 @ f5.6

Page 88: **Glacial ice river**
Canon 1Ds Mk 2 + 24–105mm
Canon; 100 ISO; 1/500 @ f8

Page 90: **Looking up at the dive hole**
Nikon F2 + 24mm Nikkor; Oceanic
housing; Subsea 150 flash;
Ektachrome 200; 1/60 @ f8

Page 91: **Diving below the iceberg**
Nikon F2 + 24mm Nikkor; Oceanic
housing; Subsea 150 flash;
Ektachrome 200; 1/60 @ f8

Page 92: **Icefish** Nikon F2 + 24mm
Nikkor; Oceanic housing; Subsea 150
flash; Ektachrome 200; 1/60 @ f11

Page 93: **Reef life** Nikon F2 + 24mm
Nikkor; Oceanic housing; Subsea 150
flash; Ektachrome 200; 1/60 @ f11

Page 93: **Feeding anemone** Nikonos
3 + 35mm lens + extension tube;
Vivitar flash; Ektachrome 64; 1/60 @ f16

Page 93: **Giant isopod** Nikonos 3 +
35mm lens + extension tube; Vivitar
flash; Ektachrome 64; 1/60 @ f16

Page 95: **Crabeater seals resting**
Canon 1Ds Mk 2 + 24–105mm Canon;
100 ISO; 1/250 @ f8; polarising filter

Page 97: **Rick with crabeaters**
Nikon F2 + 24mm Nikkor; Oceanic
housing; Subsea 150 flash;
Ektachrome 200; 1/60 @ f5.6

Page 99: **Polar bears fighting**
Nikon F90 + 80–200mm Nikkor;
Fuji Sensia 100; 1/500 @ f5.6

Page 101: **Dead cub**
Nikon F90 + 20–40mm Tamron;
Fuji Sensia 100; 1/125 @ f11

Page 102: **Red-algae snow**
Nikon F2 + 24mm Nikkor;
Ektachrome 64; 1/250 @ f11

Page 105: **Penguins, Booth Island**
Canon 1Ds Mk 2 + 100–400mm
Canon; 200 ISO; 1/500 @ f8

Page 107: **Mud-covered Adélie chick**
Nikon F2 + 80–200mm Nikkor;
Ektachrome 200; 1/500 @ f5.6

Page 109: **Polar bear footprints**
Nikon F90 + 20–40mm Tamron;
Fuji Sensia 100; 1/250 @ f11

Page 110: **Ice floes**
Canon 1Ds Mk 2 + 17–40mm Canon;
100 ISO; 1/250 @ f8; polarising filter

Page 111: **Gentoos on the last ice**
Canon G10; 100 ISO; 1/250 @ f8

Page 113: **Polar bear nose**
Canon 1Ds Mk 2 + 17–40mm Canon;
100 ISO; 1/60 @ f22

Page 115: **Light on the ice**
Canon 1Ds Mk 2 + 100–400mm
Canon; 200 ISO; 1/250 @ f5.6

Page 117: **Weddell seal and pup**
Canon 1Ds Mk 2 + 100–400mm
Canon; 200 ISO; 1/500 @ f8

Page 118: **Killer whale hunting**
Canon 1Ds Mk 2 + 100–400mm
Canon; 200 ISO; 1/500 @ f11

Page 120: **Killer whale eyeing a crabbie**
Canon 1Ds Mk 2 + 100–400mm
Canon; 200 ISO; 1/500 @ f8

Page 121: **Killer whale eyeing crabbies**
Canon 1Ds Mk 2 + 100–400mm
Canon; 400 ISO; 1/1000 @ f8

Page 122: **Killer whales spyhopping**
Canon 1Ds Mk 2 + 100–400mm
Canon; 400 ISO; 1/500 @ f8

Page 124: **Killer whale and a Weddell**
Canon 1Ds Mk 2 + 100–400mm
Canon; 200 ISO; 1/500 @ f8

Page 125: **Killers preparing to attack**
Canon 1Ds Mk 2 + 100–400mm
Canon; 400 ISO; 1/500 @ f8

Page 126: **Killer whales making waves**
Canon 1Ds Mk 2 + 100–400mm
Canon; 400 ISO; 1/1000 @ f8

Page 127 top: **Weddell hit by the wave**
Canon 1Ds Mk 2 + 100–400mm
Canon; 400 ISO; 1/1000 @ f8

Page 127 bottom: **Weddell washed off**
Canon 1Ds Mk 2 + 100–400mm
Canon; 200 ISO; 1/1000 @ f8

Page 129: **Snow petrel**
Canon 1Ds Mk 2 + 100–400mm
Canon; 200 ISO; 1/1000 @ f11

Page 130: **Snow arrow for the sub**
Canon 1Ds Mk 2 + 17–40mm Canon;
100 ISO; 1/250 @ f11

Page 131: **Submarine surfacing**
Canon G10; 100 ISO; 1/250 @ f8

Page 133: **Emperor bubble trails**
Nikonos 5 + 15mm Nikkor; Fuji Sensia
200 pushed to 400; 1/250 @ f5.6

Page 135: **Minke in the Antarctic**
Canon 1Ds Mk 2 + 17–40mm Canon;
200 ISO; 1/250 @ f5.6

Page 137: Two climbers, Illampu
Nikon FE + 24mm Nikkor; Kodachrome 64; 1/250 @ f8; polarising filter

Page 139: Skidoo under water Nikon F2 + 24mm Nikkor; Oceanic housing; Subsea flash; Ektachrome 200; 1/60 @ f8

Page 141: Diving guillemots
Nikonos 5 + 15mm Nikkor; Fuji Sensia 100 pushed to 200 ISO; 1/250 @ f8

Page 143: Crevasse ladder, Everest
Nikon FE + 24mm Nikkor; Ektachrome 100; 1/125 @ f5.6

Page 145: Crossing a crevasse, Everest
Nikon FE + 24mm Nikkor; Ektachrome 100; 1/125 @ f8

Page 147: Everest base camp
Canon 1Ds Mk 2 + 17–40mm Canon; 100 ISO; 1/250 @ f8

Page 149: Higher camp in a blizzard
Canon 1Ds Mk 2 + 17–40mm Canon; 100 ISO; 1/250 @ f11

Page 151: Line of climbers, Everest
Canon G10; 100 ISO; 1/250 @ f11

Page 153: Zavodovski island
Nikon F90 + 80–2000mm Tamron; Fuji Sensia 100; 1/250 @ f8

Page 154: Penguin colony, Zavodovski
Nikon F90 + 80–200mm Tamron; Fuji Sensia 100; 1/125 @ f8

Page 157: Chinstraps, Zavodovski
Nikon F90 + 20–40mm Tamron; Fuji Sensia 100; 1/250 @ f8

Page 159: Chinstraps on an iceberg
Nikon F90 + 80–200mm Nikkor; Fuji Sensia 100; 1/250 @ f11

Page 161: Huskies crossing a crack
Canon 1Ds Mk 2 + 17–40mm Canon; 100 ISO; 1/250 @ f8

Page 163: Arctic fox
Canon G10; 200 ISO; 1/100 @ f5.6

Page 165: Climbing into the crevasse
Nikon FE + 24mm Nikkor; Ektachrome 200; 1/60 @ f5.6

Page 167: Polar bear with a seal kill
Nikon FE + 80–200mm Nikkor; Fuji Sensia 100; 1/250 @ f11

Page 169: Ice floe break-up
Canon 1N + 17–35mm Canon; Ektachrome 100; 1/125 @ f11

Page 170: Doug on the radio
Canon 1N + 17–35mm Canon; Ektachrome 100; 1/125 @ f11

Page 170: Doug and Sue
Canon 1N + 17–35mm Canon; Ektachrome 100; 1/250 @ f8

Page 170: Loading up the helicopter
Canon 1N + 17–35mm Canon; Ektachrome 100; 1/125 @ f16

Page 171: View from the helicopter
Canon 1N + 17–35mm Canon; Ektachrome 100; 1/250 @ f11

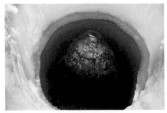

Page 173: Weddell in the dive hole
Canon 1Ds Mk 2 + 17–40mm Canon; 100 ISO; 1/250 @ f5.6

Page 175: Weddell seal mum and pup
Nikon F2 + 24mm Nikkor; Oceanic housing; Subsea 150 flash; Ektachrome 200; 1/60 @ f5.6

Page 177: Harp seal pup
Nikon F90 + 80–200mm Nikkor; Fuji Sensia 100; 1/250 @ f8

Page 179: Fur seals under water
Nikonos 5 + 15mm Nikkor; Ektachrome 200; 1/250 @ f5.6

Page 181: **Fur seal portrait**
Nikon FE + 80–200mm Nikkor; Fuji
Sensia 200; 1/250 @ f8

Page 183: **Smiley elephant seals**
Nikon F2 + 80–200mm Nikkor;
Ektachrome 200; 1/250 @ f5.6

Page 184: **Leopard seal penguin catch**
Canon 1Ds Mk 2 + 100–400mm
Canon; 200 ISO; 1/500 @ f11

Page 184: **Leopard seal flaying its prey**
Canon 1Ds Mk 2 + 100–400mm
Canon; 400 ISO; 1/1000 @ f8

Page 184: **Flayed penguin**
Canon 1Ds Mk 2 + 100–400mm
Canon; 400 ISO; 1/1000 @ f8

Page 184: **Leopard seal penguin catch**
Nikonos 5 + 15mm Nikkor;
Ektachrome 200; 1/125 @ f8

Page 185: **Leopard seal and diver**
Nikonos 5 + 15mm Nikkor;
Ektachrome 200; 1/250 @ f5.6

Page 186: **Bearded seal**
Nikon F90 + 80–200mm Nikkor;
Fuji Sensia 200; 1/250 @ f8

Page 187: **Hooded seal display**
Nikon FE + 80–200mm Nikkor;
Fuji Sensia 200; 1/250 @ f8

Page 189: **Bloody giant petrel**
Nikon F90 + 80–200mm Nikkor;
Kodachrome 64; 1/250 @ f 8

Page 191: **Adélie chick and parent**
Canon G10; 100 ISO; 1/250 @ f11

Page 193: **Jason and a polar bear**
Nikon F90 + 80–200mm Nikkor;
Fuji Sensia 100; 1/250 @ f5.6

Page 195: **Polar bear prints by a crack**
Nikon F90 + 20–40mm Tamron;
Fuji Sensia 100; 1/250 @ f11

Page 196: **Albatross pair displaying**
Nikon F90 + 20-40mm Tamron;
Fuji Sensia 100; 1/250 @ f8

Page 199: **Arctic fox and reindeer**
Canon 1Ds Mk 2 + 100–400mm
Canon; 200 ISO; 1/250 @ f8

Page 201: **Belugas under water**
Nikonos 5 + 15mm Nikkor;
Ektachrome 200; 1/125 @ f5.6

Page 203: **Roaring elephant seal**
Nikon F2 + 80–200mm Nikkor;
Ektachrome 64; 1/250 @ f8

Page 205: **Pile of elephant seals**
Nikon F90 + 80–200mm Nikkor;
Kodachrome 64; 1/250 @ f8

Page 207: **Igloo and sledge**
Canon 1Ds Mk 2 + 17–40mm Canon;
200 ISO; 1/30 @ f5.6

Page 209: **Inuit building an igloo**
Nikon F90 + 20–40mm Tamron;
Fuji Sensia 200; 1/60 @ f8

Page 211: **Inuit hunting seals**
Canon 1Ds Mk 2 + 17–40mm Canon;
100 ISO; 1/250 @ f8

Page 213: **Inuit netting little auks**
Canon 1Ds Mk 2 + 17–40mm Canon;
200 ISO; 1/1000 @ f8

Page 215: **Inuit looking for bears**
Nikon FE + 80–200mm Nikkor;
Fuji Sensia 200; 1/250 @ f8

Page 217: **Boy and head of a narwhal**
Nikon F90 + 20–40mm Tamron;
Fuji Sensia 100; 1/250 @ f8

Page 219: **Emperor penguins returning**
Nikon F90 + 80–200mm Nikkor;
Fuji Sensia 100; 1/250 @ f8

Page 220: **Emperors incubating**
Nikon F2 + 24mm Nikkor;
Ektachrome 64; 1/125 @ f8

Page 223: **Emperor penguin chick**
Nikon F2 + 80–200mm Nikkor;
Ektachrome 64; 1/250 @ f5.6

Page 225: **Emperor parents and chicks**
Nikon F2 + 80–200mm Nikkor;
Ektachrome 64; 1/250 @ f8

Page 227: **Emperor chicks in a huddle**
Nikon F2 + 35mm Nikkor;
Ektachrome 64; 1/125 @ f5.6

Page 228: **Emperor colony in spring**
Nikon F2 + 80–200mm Nikkor;
Ektachrome 64; 1/250 @ f5.6

Page 232: **Backlit emperor huddle**
Nikon F2 + 80–200mm Nikkor;
Ektachrome 200; 1/125 @ f5.6

Page 240: **Doug heading under the ice**
Canon 1Ds Mk 2 + 17–40mm Canon;
100 ISO; 1/250 @ f8

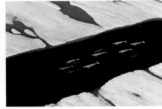

Rear endpaper: **Belugas in sea ice**
Nikon F90 + 80–200mm Nikkor; Fuji
Sensia 200; 1/125 @ f8

Published by Tartan Dragon Ltd
Photographs and text © Doug Allan 2012
Seventh printing January 2019
www.dougallan.com

Designed by Simon Bishop
Edited by Rosamund Kidman Cox
Stills colourist Stephen Johnson
Printed and bound by Akcent Media, P.O. Box 10, St. Neots, PE19 6WR
Typeset in Museo and Geometr 415

All pictures are by Doug Allan, except on pages 41, 43, 50, 168, 170
and 240, which are by Sue Flood.

ISBN 978-0-9571392-0-6

Right
Flying underwater. Penguins gave up flight in return for superb underwater adaptations. Hold this page upside down and they're like a battery of rockets taking off. In gin clear water like this off Cape Washington, they're a magic sight.

Previous page
Ice summit.
Paul, Ken and Ian from the British Antarctic Survey base on Signy Island stand on top of Wave Peak after an ascent in the winter of 1980.
This summit, almost 1000 metres high, was a popular day trip when the sea ice allowed access from Signy.

Page 1
Sunset at Churchill.
It's remarkable how the mood of bears can change while they're waiting for the ice to form. Half an hour ago, these two were up on their hind legs, pushing each other around like prizefighters. Now they're entirely relaxed and apparently the best of friends.

FREEZE FRAME

A WILDLIFE CAMERAMAN'S ADVENTURES ON ICE

DOUG ALLAN